More
Psychopaths and Love

AB ADMIN

DEDICATION

FOR YOU

TABLE OF CONTENTS

INTRODUCTION

I was victimized by a psychopath who duped me into a relationship with him. A few months after it ended, I created the website *Psychopaths and Love*. I was determined to learn all I could about what I experienced, and to share it with others who found themselves in the same predicament. I started writing and haven't stopped since.

This book is the second collection of writings from the insightful and popular blog, *Psychopaths and Love*. The essays go into more depth and detail to build upon the foundation of knowledge and self-discovery previously presented, in a unique and sometimes entertaining way.

It is divided into two sections. The first section, YOU, focuses on healing and on understanding what you experienced. The second section, THE PSYCHOPATH, focuses on understanding how the psychopathic mind works and how that can help you avoid being victimized again, or for the first time.

You can find the first collection of writings in the book, Psychopaths and Love.

SECTION ONE: YOU

1 THE REAL REASON YOU WERE VICTIMIZED BY A PSYCHOPATH

You fell for a psychopath.

You were duped, and you paid dearly. You lost time. You lost faith in others and in yourself. You experienced unimaginable grief. It's a story that will always be a part of your life.

But this story is not a story of your flaws, weaknesses, or mistakes. You didn't make mistakes. You believed in people. You trusted people to be as decent inside as you are. You trusted people to be as capable of love as you are. It is actually a story of your best qualities.

Shame is not your burden to carry. Neither is blame, from others or from yourself. What is there to feel shame for? Being a decent, loving and trusting human being? What is there to be blamed for? Being victimized by a predator, one who presented himself as being the same way?

The psychopath is the only one who deserves shame and blame.

Psychopaths target the best people. It was our best qualities — our ability to give and receive love, to trust another enough to be intimate and vulnerable, to believe in the goodness of another — that enabled them to victimize us. They clearly saw these qualities in us. Within those very qualities you find the psychopath's motives of envy, spite, and contempt. Within those very qualities you find the psychopath's ability to victimize. That can't be justified. No matter

2

what. You can not and did not cause this to happen to yourself. It is beyond the realm of explainable or acceptable human behavior. It can never be justified.

Something unimaginable, something unknown and unexpected entered our lives. A depraved imitation of a human took advantage of you, lied to you, manipulated you, used you and devalued you. Nobody ever brings that on themselves. It didn't happen because of some fault or flaw or weakness in you — it happened because of all that is good in you, and because a warped mind took that goodness and twisted it for its' own sick purpose.

That truth can be hard to understand.

I once heard the greatest gift you can give someone is the gift of being understood. Understanding is a gift….and it's one you can and should give to yourself.

Knowing why and how it happened brings understanding. With that understanding comes the recognition that you were not the one who was responsible, and the recognition that you are worthy of holding yourself in high esteem and deserving of all that is good and decent.

2 LIMINALITY, THE UNSETTLING SPACE OF IN-BETWEEN

After our experience in a psychopathic bond, we are shaken to our core. The firm foundation we believed we stood on crumbled beneath us and we hang on, barely, in any way we can.

We find ourselves in a liminal place — the place of in-between.

It is a strange place to be, and we feel fearful. But as we journey through this strange place, it changes as we change. Ultimately, it becomes the place where healing happens.

As we go through life, we have a driving unconscious desire to create a fixed and certain sense of reality. This enables us to feel safe. But all we ever really create is the illusion of it. After the psychopath, our illusions of certainty, security, and safety are shattered. We are afraid. This existential and primordial fear reaches down into the core of all that we are.

It is alarming to consider that our nicely ordered life, with its predictability and safety and certainty, actually exists on the edge of a vast and unknown wilderness.

This wilderness "is the dark aspect of the world...a place of initiation, for it is there the demonic presences and the forces of nature reveal themselves. The wilderness is the antithesis of house and heart … It holds the dark forbidden things – secrets, terrors, which threaten the protected life of the ordered world of common day," writes historian Heinrich Zimmer. We find ourselves in irreconcilable opposition between this wilderness and the civilized and familiar place we once inhabited.

Our homes and our selves are our basic places of safety. When violated, we have nowhere to go to feel safe. The fact that this violation was perpetrated by someone we thought we knew and trusted leaves us shaken and fearful. That someone could have manipulated their way into our hearts, and then continued on freely to our souls, leaves us in this liminal space.

"Liminality embodies the abject, the in-between, the ambiguous, the composite that disturbs identity, system, order," according to Teresa A. Goddu, in *Gothic America: Narrative, History and Nation*. It is a very uncomfortable place to be, to say the least.

In a state of liminality, "participants stand at the threshold between their previous way of structuring their identity…and a new way. Continuity of tradition may become uncertain, and future outcomes once taken for granted may be thrown into doubt."

We find ourselves in some kind of uncanny place that exists between 'this world' — the everyday world we thought we knew — and the other one we only recently discovered. We look around us, and on its surface everything appears the same as it did before. The sun rises, the clock ticks, the phone rings, and snow falls or flowers bloom. But there is a sense that resemblance is an uncanny one. While everything around us may appear to be the same, it has taken on the quality of having been fundamentally changed beneath the surface. Even though we look the same when we see ourselves in the mirror, we know we have been fundamentally altered in some profound way, deep beneath our skin.

This uncanny aspect extends into the very way we see things. We may give way to superstitious beliefs. According to Sartre, magic is dominant when control over our experience is weak. "Magical beliefs and the fearful reactions based on such beliefs are the result of the state of uncertainty we are in, created by this challenge and by the negation of our expectations. Our feelings come from the conviction of loss of control and the sense of helplessness we feel when our cognitive system can neither assimilate our experience into its own structure nor adapt itself to the structure of the experience."

What we believed was real and solid now seems like nothing but a house of cards that was ready to be blown over by a strong enough wind. The psychopath was that wind.

Thomas L. Dumm pointed out that "Fear once meant the experience of being between places of protection, in transit, in a situation analogous to the condition that is commonly referred as liminality." This idea of being in between places of safety applies equally well to paradigms of thought as it does to physical places, and it helps to explain the sense of uncanniness and fear we feel. We journeyed outside our usual paradigm and into an alternate one that we never even knew existed.

A key feature of liminality is the stage of reintegration. When this reintegration does not happen, liminality becomes permanent, which can be very dangerous. Only when we can take that new paradigm, and accept it and integrate it with our old one, does our fear and our sense of the uncanny resolve.

A reader named 'Aurora' explained it beautifully:

"This...explains exactly how I was feeling a year ago. It's a terribly frightening place, and I remember distinctly feeling like the ground was unsteady under my feet. The things that were previously precious and meaningful to me suddenly made no sense at all. It was a spiritual crisis, as well as an emotional and physical one.

I haven't read a better description of this 'space' one finds oneself in after having had an experience with a psychopath. It really is a strange and barren landscape and it takes time and self care to get back to a space of feeling safe – safe emotionally deep within the self, within ones own home, thoughts, identity, reality, within one's community and within ones sense of reality and trust.

I still have a long way to go with this, but I feel now I know more fully what I am dealing with. I no longer let wishful thinking, nostalgia or cognitive dissonance dull the painful but necessary task of facing the reality of what happened to me. It can be truly transforming, but is it a journey, and one where it is so important to get the help you need, and those that truly understand just how many levels the pain infiltrates."

~

Liminality is brought about by trauma and tragedy. It is the space of transition. It is also the space of transformation.

3 YOUR JOURNEY IS THE HERO'S JOURNEY

"You are the hero of your own story."

~Joseph Campbell

Recovery from involvement in a psychopathic bond was a long and rocky road. But in the arduous process of healing after it was over, I discovered some things within myself that I didn't know were there: Resilience. The strength to overcome adversity. The ability to put myself first. You will also discover surprising things about yourself.

While you maneuver the unpredictable jungle of memories, realizations and emotions, it is your spirit that you face head on, and you may be astounded by what you find: A hero.

One day you will be able to take the very big step of having this become a story in your life rather than the story of your life. It is an important and unforgettable story, a life-changing one, and an archetypal story in so many ways: It's the hero's journey. You can re-frame your experience in this way, if you choose to, when you're ready. In the aftermath, I had a conversation with a very skilled therapist who took my story and put it in the context of the archetypal hero's journey, and it helped to shift my mindset to a more positive one that helped me move forward. I hope it will do the same for you, or that you will find your own source of inspiration and determination.

What is the hero's journey?

"A hero ventures forth from the world of common day into a region of supernatural wonder: forces are there encountered and a decisive victory is won: the hero comes back from this mysterious adventure with the power to bestow boons on his fellow man." ~ Joseph Campbell

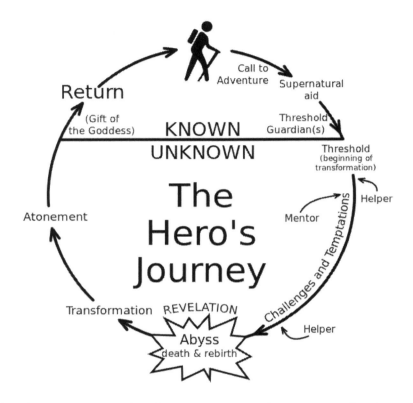

The hero's journey is about growth and passage. The journey requires an experience that causes a separation from your comfortable, everyday world of the past, one that ultimately causes initiation into a new level of awareness and skill, and then a return back home.

There are three stages to the hero's journey: Departure, when you left your familiar world and journeyed into the dark unknown; Initiation, when you were subjected to a series of great trials, both during and after; and Return, when you 'come back home' with your new wisdom and strengths and the "Freedom to Live," which marks your attainment of psychological freedom from the psychopath.

At some point, it may be helpful to substitute in your mind the stages of the hero's journey — Departure, Initiation, and Return – in place of the stages of the pathological bond — Idealize, Devalue, Discard. This may help you to re-frame your experience in a way that helps you to move forward.

You will know when you're ready to do this. It probably won't be early on; most likely it will be when some time has passed and you realize the strength it took to get through the experience, when you're ready to take a stand for yourself and say in one way or another "I have worth and I will not let what that person did affect me and my life in a negative way any longer." It's a mental shift that happens, one that changes your perspective and gives strong energy. It may be the point of going from victim to survivor.

But even a hero needs some help.

"Oftentimes the hero must have powerful guides and rescuers to bring them back to everyday life, especially if the person has been wounded or weakened by the experience."

I hope you will find whatever help you need, both from within and without, to make your return back home.

"It is by going down into the abyss that we recover the treasures of life."

~Joseph Campbell

4 POST-TRAUMATIC GROWTH

Writing about the hero's journey inspired me to continue with this positive theme and talk about Post-Traumatic Growth (PTG).

"Trauma creates a rupture in a person's life story. Assumptions about ourselves, our place in world, and our expectations about the world are shaken, even shattered," says Stephen Joseph, Ph.D.

I think many of us would agree that he summed it up very well. It can be hard to believe that anything good can come of this, until you understand or experience PTG.

What is PTG? Post-traumatic growth happens when adversity leads us to a new and more meaningful life, one where we re-evaluate our priorities, deepen relationships, and come to a new understanding of who we are. Post-traumatic growth goes beyond coping. It's about "changes that cut to the very core of our way of being in the world."

You may feel at this point that your ordeal was too terrible to ever recover from, and that going even further to experience positive growth from it is out of the question. But it is possible. PTG does not suggest that you aren't suffering as your wisdom grows. In fact, significant distress might be necessary for PTG to occur. Research shows a correlation between PTSD (post-traumatic stress disorder) and PTG, "suggesting that the disruption caused by the trauma is significant enough to create psychiatric symptoms and "shattering" enough to your "assumptive world view" to generate growth. (Melinda Moore, "Positive Changes in the Aftermath of Crisis")

Martin Seligman, director of the Positive Psychology Center at the University of Pennsylvania, says "Very often, extremely bad events lead to personal and moral dilemmas. And they're existential crises in which you have to make decisions. We talk about it as a fork in the road. One of the most interesting things about depression, which is the big, big component of post traumatic stress disorder, it is an emotion that tells you to detach from goals you had. That they're unreachable. And that creates a fork in the road. It makes you ask the question, what other things might I do? What doors might open for me?"

What are the top things expressed by people who have experienced PTG? According to Jane McGonigal in her TED talk "Gaming Can Make a Better World," they say the following:

"My priorities have changed. I'm not afraid to do what makes me happy. I feel closer to my friends and family. I understand myself better. I know who I really am now. I have a new sense of meaning and purpose in my life. I'm better able to focus on my goals and dreams."

May you experience post-traumatic GROWTH.

5 You Did Not Participate in Your Own Exploitation

A friend brought to my attention a post on a related website asserting that "when we become romantically involved with a sociopath we *participate,* in one way or another, in our own exploitation."

(jaw drops)

The author states that we 'participate' because we "believe what we want to believe," such as "everyone is good inside" or "everybody just wants to be loved" or "with love, anything is possible." She goes on to say that these beliefs conflict with the things we don't want to believe, such as "warnings from everyone we know…that the person is bad news."

I consider the beliefs mentioned above to be normal…until you've been a victim. Having had these normal beliefs does not mean you participated in your exploitation.

I think the correct description is that *we believed what we were manipulated to believe*, which aligned with what we wanted because the manipulator figured out what we longed for, and then pretended to be just that. It's the crux of what they do.

The problem isn't your beliefs, or your friends warning you or not, or *you* — the problem is that there are predators who are skilled manipulators.

Those of you who are familiar with my blog or books know I am all for learning about what happened, learning what we were dealing with, and finding out what we might do to avoid being re-victimized. But I have never conveyed the message that we 'participated' in our own exploitation. Why? Because it's not true. I take issue with this idea and I feel it takes a victim-blaming stance, even if the author didn't intend it.

No one would knowingly participate in psychopathic victimization. We were psychologically manipulated. The predator took advantage of our human nature. This manipulation caused us to believe he or she loved us, and then caused us to doubt ourselves and doubt our doubts about them.

par·tic·i·pa·tion
noun
the action of taking part in something.

Participation implies active involvement. In the case of a person involved with a psychopath, that implies knowledge of what was going on but forging ahead anyway.

But in truth, what causes us to become involved is a LACK of knowledge of what is really happening, brought about by manipulation.

"Psychological manipulation is a type of social influence that aims to change the perception or behavior of others through underhanded, deceptive, or even abusive tactics."

~ Wikipedia

So how can we participate in something we don't know is happening? How do we participate in our own exploitation if we are not aware of it?

And if we were aware, why the hell would we?

The blog author also said, "And if we believed in listening to ourselves, we may be more willing to pay attention when our intuition is warning us to get away from someone."

Intuition? You mean that thing psychopaths are so adept at disarming, just when we need it most?

Mary Ellen O'Toole, PhD, the author of "Dangerous Instincts," a former senior FBI analyst who now teaches FBI agents and other law enforcement about psychopaths, says that they are able to disarm our intuition — and that's precisely what makes them so dangerous.

The view that victims participated in their own exploitation is deeply harmful. It perpetuates ignorance about predators, and it perpetuates shame and victim-blaming. I'm shocked to see it on a website many victims turn to when they need help. This attitude will do nothing to help someone heal, and everything to continue the abuse long after the perpetrator is gone.

We did not try to turn a frog into a prince -- It was the prince who turned into a frog, after all.

6 FALLING INTO A PARALLEL UNIVERSE

Psychopathy is a wildly popular subject. Psychopathic characters are portrayed in movies and on TV. Best-selling books revolve around them. In reams of articles, we hear about psychopaths as serial killers, CEOs and those who work on Wall Street and in government.

But at the same time, we hear nothing about psychopaths in personal, one-on-one relationships.

Often, we even hear that psychopaths don't really exist at all.

Where does that leave us, the up-close-and-personal victims of psychopaths? Out of luck, that's where. Except in books and on websites like this one, out in the fringes of cyberspace, where we are driven to find information, validation and support.

When we go about our lives and then unwittingly step into the lair of a psychopath, it seems we enter a parallel universe. We are unsuspecting, due to the information that is withheld or that remains unknown. And when we emerge on the other side, battered and broken, there is little there to help us.

Psychopathy has been a subject of controversy for well over a century within the mental health community. And because of that, it is also a subject of controversy amongst our friends and family — and even amongst the psychotherapists we seek for help — who think we must be crazy when we tell them what happened to us. They've heard of psychopathy and they've read about it and are even enthralled by it, but they will not believe we were intimately involved with a psychopath.

Even with the commonly cited statistic that one out of a hundred is a psychopath, it is somehow unbelievable that we could have been involved in a relationship with a psychopath. No one believes us. Not our friends and not the therapists we reach out to for help in the aftermath. Our friends can sometimes be excused. But many of us visited mental health professionals who knew nothing about psychopathy, as if they lived in a vacuum.

"Many therapists simply don't appreciate the kinds of unique trauma folks currently in or who have survived toxic relationships have experienced. And at times, a therapist might even misinterpret the results of their initial screening and assessment of a victim. Folks who've been traumatized might appear a certain way upon examination that doesn't really reflect the kind of person they really are, or at least who they were before adapting to their trauma (they're even likely to perform differently than they would otherwise perform on various psychological assessment instruments they might be given). So whether a therapist is working with a current victim or a survivor, they need to know how the character disturbed individual's behaviors and tactics have likely impacted the victim and affected their current level of functioning." Dr. George Simon, 'Getting the Right Kind of Help, Part II'

Then we learn there is no actual diagnosis of psychopathy in the DSM, the diagnostic bible of psychiatry, and that it has instead been mixed in with antisocial personality disorder. Yes, psychopaths are antisocial, but not always in the ways characterized by the diagnosis of ASPD, and not for the same reasons. While psychopathy may have some things in common with ASPD, they are two completely different things.

"Researchers who were influential in developing the modern DSM argued that the diagnosis should be based mainly on observable patterns of behavior rather than psychological constructs. And so, ASPD emphasizes aggressive behavior, rule-breaking, and criminal acts. Not surprisingly, 80–90 percent of inmates in maximum-security prisons meet criteria for ASPD, though only 15–20 percent qualify as psychopaths." Dr. Jordan Smoller, associate vice chair of the MGH Department of Psychiatry and professor of psychiatry at Harvard Medical School

Oh, so it should be based on "mainly observable patterns..." Observable by whom? Not by us, that's for sure. That doesn't count. But who is there to observe a psychopath in a personal relationship? No one...except us.

"Virtually all of the research done in psychopathy is on the perpetrators, and we tend to ignore the tens of thousands of victims of these individuals. And most of the victims have nowhere to turn. They talk to their psychiatrist, psychologist, their friends, their employees, their priest, and they get nowhere because most people don't understand the nature of psychopathic people."

From the video, "Dr. Robert Hare, Sponsor of Aftermath"

We fell through the cracks, and ended up in a parallel universe. And it adds to the damage done to us by the perpetrators — psychopaths. Yes, they really do exist. And yes, they date and even marry. Even though there's not always a psychiatrist there to observe it.

7 THE HIDDEN VULNERABILITY WE ALL HAVE, REVEALED

There are many things that leave us vulnerable to predatory manipulators. But no discussion of what may make us vulnerable is complete without revealing one vulnerability we *all* have, but that remains hidden from us.

We see others and the world through it, as if we were wearing a pair of distorted lenses, yet we don't even know we have those glasses on.

But guess what? Manipulators know all about it, and they use it to their advantage with great success. What is this hidden vulnerability?

Our brains work in an automatic way much of the time. This automatic 'shortcut' function built into our brain is called Cognitive Bias. These biases leave us vulnerable, because they often lead us to make faulty assumptions and come to incorrect conclusions.

One bias is called 'selective attention,' which keeps us from consciously seeing unexpected things. We selectively pick out one message from a mixture of messages occurring at the same time. Our brain edits out certain things because there's just too much coming at us to consider it all consciously, and it goes with what's familiar. There's a famous psychology video that asks the viewer to count how many times a group of people passes a basketball. After giving our answer, we find out a person in a gorilla suit walked right through the basketball players, right in front of our eyes; yet most of us didn't see it. When we watch the video again knowing it's there, we are shocked that we could have missed it. It's unbelievable.

Cognitive biases are part of the reason we didn't 'see' the psychopath, who was a big gorilla right in front of us.

According to the University at Albany,

"Although cognitive biases can sometimes be helpful in familiar situations or in dealing with predictable threats, *they can lead to catastrophic failures in assessment of unfamiliar and unpredictable adversaries.*"

Isn't that the truth? Getting involved with a psychopath was nowhere on our radar. It was unfamiliar and unpredictable.

The human mind has evolved to have and use many different automatic shortcuts and to generate all kinds of assumptions. We all do these things unconsciously, by virtue of being human.

Here's a list of some of the biases that may have made us vulnerable to that "unfamiliar and unpredictable adversary":

Projection Bias or Assumed Similarity Bias (not to be confused with psychological "projecting"): This mental shortcut leads us to the unconscious assumption that others share the same or similar values, thoughts and beliefs. In other words, we believe that others are just like us. If we are an honest, loving and kind person with a conscience, we believe most everyone else is the same way. We don't even consider that some people may have drastically different values and motivations.

The Affect Heuristic: This is a mental shortcut that allows a strong emotional first impression to affect decisions, even if subsequent evidence weighs against the original decision. First impressions often remain even after the evidence on which they are based has been totally discredited. This bias is described as "going with your gut instinct," which may not always be the best thing to do. The psychopath creates a great first impression, and we get stuck on that.

The Just-World Hypothesis or Just-World Fallacy: This is the cognitive bias (or assumption) that "a person's actions always bring morally fair and fitting consequences to that person, so that all noble actions are eventually rewarded and all evil actions are eventually punished." This means if we see ourselves as a good person, we believe only good things will happen to us. We just don't expect that something bad may happen, so we're not even looking for it. (Because this bias also includes the belief that people "get what they deserve," it is at the root of victim blaming.)

The Observer's Illusion Of Transparency: This one causes us to overestimate how well we understand another person's personal mental states. We assume we know what someone else is thinking and feeling, when in fact we don't.

The Confirmation Bias: This is the tendency to search for, interpret, focus on and remember information in a way that confirms our preconceptions. This makes it hard to change your mind about something — or someone — once you've already developed a belief about who they are. If someone has already won you over and gained your trust, it is very hard to change that perception, even when things start to go very wrong.

About the confirmation bias, from the Psychology Today article, "4 Reasons You Can't Trust Yourself":

"Would you use the following words or phrases to describe yourself when you make a decision or take a position for or against something?

Open-minded
Good judge of the facts
Attentive to reason
Skilled at evaluating an argument

Sadly, this list is pretty much science fiction because of the confirmation bias, one of the many shortcuts the brain takes which leaves us thinking "fast," and pretty much automatically, rather than carefully processing. Research shows that instead of judging and weighing all the facts, we listen to and give credence to those facts and arguments that align with or reflect beliefs we already hold. I'm sure you're shaking your head and saying, "Not me!" as you read this. Sorry; there's no point in your fooling yourself."

The granddaddy of all biases is The Bias Blind Spot: People are largely blind to their own cognitive biases. We will accept that biases exist in others, but tend to deny that we ourselves have biases.

So what, if anything, can we do to think logically and objectively and override our brain's automatic shortcuts and assumptions?

There is no easy answer or any easy way to do this, but plenty of people are working on it. Awareness may help.

In his book *Thinking, Fast and Slow*, Daniel Kahneman argues that if we consciously identify and attend to our biases in real-time (a feat that requires great effort) we can lessen their affect on our reasoning, to some degree.

But Alex Lickerman, M.D., believes attending to our biases isn't enough. He says the remedy is mindfulness, or taking the time and expending the energy "to examine our own thought processes consciously and continuously." And he says that must include trying to question our assumptions, too, although that's difficult because we are often unaware of them, just as we are often unaware of our cognitive biases.

8 DO YOU MAKE THIS SIMPLE (BUT DANGEROUS) MISTAKE ABOUT THE PSYCHOPATHIC MIND?

"Misinterpreting the behavior of a disordered character is the first step in the process of being victimized by them."

~ Dr. George Simon

Previously, I wrote about errors in our thinking called cognitive biases, those automatic ways our minds work that keep us from seeing things clearly. One of those biases is the Assumed Similarity Bias — a mental shortcut that leads us to the unconscious assumption that others share the same or similar values, thoughts and beliefs. We automatically assume that others are just like we are, especially when it comes to the fundamental aspects of our characters that are so basic we never even give them a second thought — such as having a conscience.

In other words, you never for a moment stop to consider that some people in fact have a drastically different way of being, one that is so foreign to you that you can't even begin to grasp it.

Even though you may have read many times that psychopaths have no conscience, no empathy, no guilt, no remorse, no shame, and no ability to love...and even after all you've been through in your experience with such a person...you may still not be able to grasp the truth of what this means, or truly understand just how fundamentally different they are.

Until you do, you are at greater risk. At greater risk of 'reconciling' with the person who victimized you. At greater risk of having a new manipulator come into your life. And at greater risk of not truly understanding what you experienced, which will complicate and slow your recovery.

As an example, here's a recent comment I got from a reader:

"Why does a psychopath depend on the love of others? Because he fears his emptiness, isn't it?...He searches for people to cling to...There MUST be some vulnerability deep down at that spot, otherwise he wouldn't get angry...he is just not able to make a life with an authentic purpose..."

My response:

"He doesn't depend on our love because he 'fears emptiness'...he depends on it because our love enables him to exploit and manipulate us. He doesn't search for people to 'cling to,' he searches for people to victimize. Don't forget, we are dealing with a predator. You are attributing your feelings and motivations to him, when in fact they are not like yours at all. The anger is simply from frustration when he doesn't get his needs met. They do not share our need for 'authentic purpose.' That's your need, not the need of the psychopath. They have their own purpose, which is vastly different from your purpose."

How can a lack of understanding affect your recovery?

Well, you might still have the belief that you were at fault for a promising relationship having gone wrong. You might internalize his lies that it was you who made mistakes or who didn't give enough or love enough. You might think that you want another chance to try again, try harder, and so you might get back together with him. You might feel that love and acceptance have the power to change anyone, and berate yourself for falling short. You might hear that he met someone else and married her just a short while later, and in addition to being crushed, you'll wonder what she had that you didn't.

If your ex was truly psychopathic, none of this is true. It is Simply. Not. Possible.

"As hard as it is to imagine, there are individuals with no conscience at all. It's so hard to imagine that it's one of the main reasons such people are able to prey upon others. No one can believe that the person they've been dealing with is as heartless or remorseless as they suspect."

~ Dr George Simon, PhD, "Personal Empowerment: Let Go of Harmful Misconceptions"

When we experience someone engaging in bad behavior of one kind or another, we think of it in terms of why WE might act that way and how WE would feel afterward. When we do this, we come up with the idea that the behavior may stem from insecurity, past wounds, fear, or a lack of love; and we imagine they must feel shame and guilt after treating us so badly. Because of this, we are more apt to forgive, to let things slide, to stick it out and see if things will change with love and acceptance and time.

But when the same things happen again and again, it comes time to face an important truth:

The only intelligent way to make judgments about people is to base those judgments on their patterns of behavior, and not on what we think the reasons for their behavior might be, according to Simon.

"The single most important empowerment tool is to 'accept no excuses' for hurtful, harmful, or inappropriate behavior."

~Dr. George Simon

I will no longer try to explain or understand anyone's bad behavior. This is now one of my boundaries: I will accept no excuses for hurtful, harmful or deceitful behavior.

Unfortunately, traditional psychology still hangs on to the outdated belief that everyone is struggling with insecurities and fears, and teaches that this struggle is what causes problem behavior. This puts us at a disadvantage and leaves us vulnerable to abuse and exploitation. And it seems to say that the field of psychology itself is operating under its own 'assumed similarity' bias!

My own therapist had difficulty accepting the facts of how the psychopathic mind works, which was due to her 'humanistic' perspective. Humanistic psychology is founded on the principles that all people are inherently good and have a drive toward self-actualization, and that ethical values are strong psychological forces that are one of the basic determinants of human behavior. It advocates an unconditional positive regard for everyone. Empathy is one of the most important aspects, so the therapist must have the ability to see the world through the eyes of the patient.

Although this humanistic approach sounds wonderful (and it truly would be, in a perfect world), my therapist's quest to accept everyone (by seeing them as fundamentally the same) actually caused her to completely exclude two groups of people — psychopaths and their victims. She was basically denying the very existence of psychopathic people, and therefore by default invalidating me as well. That didn't feel very humanistic to me.

I let her know that she could not see the world through my eyes — meaning she could not be truly empathetic and could not help me — unless she understood what I had experienced, and that in order to do that, she needed to understand how the mind of a psychopath worked. This was an extraordinarily empathetic and genuine woman (which in and of itself was extremely therapeutic for me at that time) who had a sincere desire to help others and be the best therapist she could possibly be, so she took the time and effort to read and learn, and she came to understand the truth.

It's very difficult to understand how the psychopathic mind works because it is so totally different from what we know. I think it's made even harder because we don't want to believe it's possible, and we don't want to accept that the person we were involved with was not at all who or what we thought they were, and that nothing we believed about the relationship was true. But it is important to understand so you can truly grasp what you experienced. It will help you move forward in your recovery, and what you learn from it can protect you from further victimization.

9 Never Trust Your Gut...Unless it Tells You to RUN

"Always trust your gut."

That's what common wisdom tells us. We've got our built-in Spidey Sense working behind the scenes to protect us, if only we would listen. We've got our Bat Girl or Bat Boy Glasses on, ready to spot the first hint of potential trouble. Or...maybe not.

Victims of all kinds are often blamed for not listening to their intuition or for ignoring their "gut instincts." Surely we must have known! It would have never happened to them. We even end up blaming ourselves.

So what happened? Where were our gut instincts when we needed them? And if they did sound the alarm, why didn't we listen?

Psychopaths are very good at disarming our gut instincts. Sometimes, our alarm bells never go off at all. Even if we do have a bad "gut feeling," they're skilled at getting us to let down our guard and push our doubts aside.

Many of us have experienced this, or we wouldn't be here reading this. I've heard many former victims berate themselves for not listening to their gut feelings. They either say they did have a bad feeling but ignored it, or they never got bad vibes at all, which they blame on being "out of touch" with their intuition. *These ideas point to a fundamental lack of understanding about what manipulation really is and how it works.* When someone says, "I just didn't listen to my intuition, but next time I will," it means they're still at risk.

Our 'guts' are not reliable indicators of danger or safety. I'm not suggesting that if you have a bad gut feeling about something, you should ignore it. Not at all — that would be foolish. As the title says, "Never Trust Your Gut...Unless it Tells You To Run." This article is about what to do when your gut stays neutral or when it gives the "all clear." No one's gut is right 100% of the time. It's not reliable enough to base your safety on.

Our gut feelings aren't some magical, mysterious, and infallible ability we're born with. In reality, gut feelings are based on our knowledge and experience. Gut feelings are sudden, strong judgments whose origin we can't seem to explain. To us, they seem to emerge from a mysterious inner force, but they don't. Cognitive science found they actually begin with a perception of something outside ourselves, like a facial expression or a tone of voice. From there, our brain goes into a mode of using its built-in shortcuts. Intuition is an unconscious and super-fast associative process in which your brain takes in a situation, does a quick search of its files, and then finds its best match among all of your stored memories and knowledge. Based on what it finds, you ascribe meaning to the situation in front of you.

An expert who believes she can tell us if we should trust our intuition or not is Mary Ellen O'Toole, Ph.D. , one of the most senior profilers for the FBI until her retirement in 2009. She has helped capture, interview and understand some of the world's most infamous serial killers. O'Toole worked on such cases as the Green River Killer, the Elizabeth Smart kidnapping and the hunt for the Unabomber. She is recognized as the FBI's leading expert in psychopathy, and is at the forefront of mental health and law enforcement efforts to apply the concepts of psychopathy to both violent and white collar offenders. She lectures internationally on the application of the theory of psychopathy to real life situations. She gives lectures on psychopathy at the FBI Academy. She is a Fellow with the American Academy of Forensic Sciences. So we may want to listen and consider her point of view when she tells us not to trust our guts.

O'Toole gives 10 reasons why our gut instincts may be wrong. Here are a few of those reasons:

Dangerous people know how to manipulate your gut feelings. She gives the example of Bernie Madoff, who "disarmed potential investors with his charm. He impressed them with his career accomplishments and lulled them with glowing recommendations from other investors who were also unknowingly being conned."

Dangerous people can be much better at reading you than you are at reading them. O'Toole says if you are lonely, for instance, "they will listen and offer their companionship. If you suffer from low self-esteem, they will compliment you and make you feel good about yourself. They know how to get you to feel good about them, even when you shouldn't."

Our guts cause us to let down our guard for the wrong reasons. She says our guts often cause us to trust people based on superficial details that usually have little to do with true normalcy. "We trust people who look and dress like us, who share our opinions, and who fit in. Dangerous people know this, so they are often masters at appearing normal and likeable and at mirroring our values, likes and dislikes. They dress nicely and keep their houses presentable. Their behavior doesn't cause internal bells and whistles to go off."

Our guts lead us to distrust people for the wrong reasons. "We generally distrust people based on superficial details, too. This is why we often assume that straggly-haired strangers — especially the ones who are socially inept, off-putting and shifty eyed—pose the greatest threat to us. In reality, some of the oddest-looking people pose little to no harm at all."

Our guts encourage us to overlook signs of danger. "Even when the rational signs of danger are evident, it's our natural inclination to rationalize them away. For instance, you might see a small child screaming in the middle of an airport. You might ignore the child because your gut tells you, "His mother must be somewhere."

"The man sitting in front of Mary Ellen O'Toole was, she says, a well-mannered guy. "He was low-key. He was nice. He didn't swear." He was very proud of his work, which he described in polite, pleasant tones.

His name was Gary Ridgway. His other name was the Green River Killer. His work was killing at least 49 women in Washington state throughout the 1980s and 1990s. He did it all while maintaining marriages, parenting, and church-going, and he seemed very much the word neighbors often use to describe men who turn out to have headless torsos in their freezers. Which is to say, he seemed very, very nice."

~ 'Dangerous Instincts': FBI profiler explains the dangers of that 'nice' neighbor.

O'Toole found that the most dangerous criminals are often the ones who come across as the most harmless. That's how they're able to continue harming people. She says we put ourselves in physical or emotional danger in dozens of ways every day, from online dating to having someone come to our home to do repairs to hiring a financial planner.

So what should we do? Should we be paranoid and mistrustful of everyone all the time, especially when our guts tell us all is well?

No, says O'Toole. Since our gut feelings aren't reliable, we need to have another system in place.

Instead of reacting instinctively, she suggests that we follow a process she developed to evaluate threat levels from people and situations over her years with the FBI. She calls the process "SMART:" an acronym for "sound method of assessing and recognizing trouble." She lays out this method in detail in her book, *Dangerous Instincts: Use an FBI Profiler's Tactics to Avoid Unsafe Situations*. Her SMART method teaches you how to determine the true risk any given situation poses, although nothing is foolproof.

When I read this book last year, to tell you the truth I thought she was the most paranoid person on the face of the earth, and I still don't follow her advice in every situation…but I should. In light of her experience as an FBI profiler, I can understand her mindset and her wisdom. Using the same type of questioning she teaches to law enforcement, she says we can learn to evaluate boyfriends, contractors, employees, nannies and the like. "This gives people the ability to be their own FBI profiler in everyday life."

Let's say you've recovered enough to feel ready to do some online dating. How do you assess someone's online profile, and what questions should you ask? Here's an example:

"Brad's profile catches your eye right off. He describes himself as "fit and good-looking," and says, "I'm looking for the perfect soul mate I can love forever, someone who will love and take care of me." O'Toole writes about the case of William Michael Barber (the "Don Juan of con") who romanced victims via dating sites, married them, cleaned out their bank accounts, and then disappeared.

Back to Brad's profile. There are negative behaviors to watch out for. "If you're going to be online dating, look at the words in profiles," she says. Look for lots of I/me statements that could indicate narcissism. And, from the above profile, the guy describing himself as good-looking could be a narcissist, she says. (She also points out that his adoring niece might have written his profile.) Plus, your own vulnerabilities can color your perception of him. If you ignore his initial neediness because you love that he's always calling and texting to tell you how beautiful you are, you might wake up five years later with a possessive, jealous husband and think it's a sudden change, O'Toole says. Watch for patterns of behavior or hints about how he acted in past relationships. A line like "I'm not a game-player," is a red flag. Perhaps, she says, someone else has accused him of that.

Questions she suggests asking include: "What are your biggest concerns about meeting people online?" "When you've had good dating experiences, how did they go?" "When you've had bad dating experiences, how did those go?" She points out that if he blames all bad dates on the women involved, that's a red flag.

As one victim said,

"You're not getting it. A con man tells you what you want to hear. There's no reason to have a gut feeling."

10 SHAME, A FESTERING WOUND OF THE SOUL

Shame. It's the core of our experience with a psychopath. We experience shame when we're with a psychopath, and we experience shame when it's over.

Psychopaths are experts at shaming us in so many ways. Even after they're gone, the shame continues as we wonder how we allowed ourselves to be treated so poorly, how we accepted less and less until there was nothing good left, but still couldn't let go.

When our involvement with a psychopath started, it seemed like the best thing that ever happened to us. Finally, we were truly loved and appreciated (or o we thought). But then something terrible began to happen. As time went on, it seemed our faults and weaknesses made us unworthy of that love. Being slowly and painfully judged, rejected, and found unworthy by the one who loved us, and whom we loved, led us to feel deep shame.

But now you know you were manipulated, so you know you didn't deserve the shame you were made to feel. For that very same reason, you don't deserve the shame you're feeling now, for being duped. When you get that, you take a giant step forward.

What is shame?

Shame is the feeling of deep humiliation not for what we've *done,* but for what we *are.*

Shame can destroy lives. It damages your self-worth, and it's hard to live a good life when your self-worth is non-existent.

When we feel comfortable enough to take risks and expose ourselves emotionally to someone we believe we can trust — and then experience judgment and rejection instead of empathy and acceptance — we feel shame.

What heals shame?

"Empathy is the antidote to shame. The two most powerful words when we're in struggle: Me, too."

~ Brene Brown

Empathy is something we did not, and could not, get from the psychopath. And empathy is exactly what is needed now to heal from the harm done by that lack of empathy we experienced.

That's why validation is so important for a victim. And that's why victim-blaming is so damaging, whether it comes from someone else or from yourself.

Things like, *"how could you be so stupid?"* or *"how could I be so stupid?"* are devoid of empathy. They are also devoid of any understanding of how psychopathic manipulation works, which is why it's vital to learn how you were victimized. If you understand that, you will not blame yourself any longer. When the blame is gone, the shame goes right along with it.

"Dark forces are no match for the light of love, acceptance, self-respect and, most of all, courage. Truth, courage and love of oneself bring shame into the light, where it cannot survive. Love of self, self-forgiveness and the pursuit of emotional healing are soul-affirming, the universal elixir to the cancerous condition of shame."

~ Ross Rosenberg, MEd, LCPC, CADC

11 Should You Forgive the Psychopath?

"Norms of forgiveness seem unduly to burden the oppressed."

- Nancy A. Stanlick, Florida Philosophical Review, Summer 2010, 'Reconciling with Harm: An Alternative to Forgiveness and Revenge'

Forgiveness. It's what good people should do, right? We're told that forgiveness is the only way to get rid of feelings of anger and animosity. We're told that forgiveness acknowledges our recognition and acceptance of the imperfections we and every other human being have. We're told that if we choose not to forgive the abuser, there's something wrong with *us*.

There are many arguments in favor of forgiveness, but are they valid? And I don't mean valid to your mother or your pastor or your best friend, but to you.

I'm not advocating that you remain angry and bitter for the rest of your life. What I'm saying is that forgiveness is not the only way to let go of the anger. There are other ways, and they don't require us to pardon the abuser if we are opposed to that.

This is a good time to recall some of our basic human rights, many of which we seemed to have abandoned or forgotten while involved in a pathological relationship:

• I have the right to have my needs and feelings be as important as anyone else's.

- I have the right to experience and express my feelings, if I choose to do so.
- I have the right to express my opinions, if I choose to do so.
- I have the right to set my own priorities.

In light of these basic rights, the issue of forgiveness might just be the perfect place to start putting these rights into practice.

Why do I say that? Because a large part of healing is learning to acknowledge and trust our own feelings, preferences and choices again, instead of letting others dictate to us what we 'should' feel and what we 'should' do. We've all had enough of that kind of manipulation. So why let it continue with the issue of forgiveness?

"In the process of recovery, most people do not mention forgiveness as part of their progress" ~ *Stanlick*

Now if you do choose to forgive, if that helps you heal, then of course go right ahead. This article is written for those who don't feel the offender deserves forgiveness, or who feel pressured to forgive, or who feels like they must forgive to please others, or who feel anxiety over their inability to forgive, or who feel like they 'should' forgive…but just feel something is holding them back.

"Feeling miserable is compatible with forgiving someone while lamenting the fact that harm was done." ~ *Stanlick*

There is a pervasive idea that we have to forgive everyone all the time, and if we don't, there's something wrong with us. It's as if a victim doesn't have enough to deal with already. We have more than enough to handle in overcoming our victimization and the results of it, and then we are victimized yet again by the Forgiveness Brigade that wants us to believe it's something vital that we must do, for whatever their reason.

We already let the manipulator talk us out of trusting our feelings and tell us our feelings and opinions weren't valid; are we now going to let others tell us that our feelings are wrong and that we're at fault for having them? I'm not buying that. My feelings at the time were "Don't tell me how to feel, don't tell me my feelings are unacceptable, and don't tell me what I should do with them." Personally, I had enough of being manipulated, and being told I should forgive just felt like more manipulation.

I believe it's is far more therapeutic to refuse to forgive if you don't want to — after all, we were controlled by this person who harmed us, and now we're working toward getting our independence and our own voice back — so why should we again be controlled by others, who are now admonishing us to forgive? *It seems so virtuous, so we don't see it for what it really is.*

Some things are simply beyond forgiveness, and we will each decide what that means based on our own personal experience. In time, many of us — myself included — simply became indifferent. Forgiveness was not warranted, nor was it necessary for healing to occur. Nor did I even want to do it.

"A severely harmed person may have no interest in forgiving…she recognizes that as a harmed person she may still lack trust, feel violated, and suffer continuing harms as a result of the initial harm done to her. In such cases, there may come a time at which the perpetrator becomes irrelevant in her personal odyssey in experiencing harm, reacting to it, and finding a way to rebuild a life shattered or imperiled by harm." ~ Stanlick

If you choose not to forgive this particular person in this particular situation, it doesn't mean you're an unforgiving, hard-hearted person who never forgives anyone. There are plenty of reasons you may not want to forgive the person who victimized you. Maybe you don't feel he deserves it because of the magnitude of what he did to you, or because she didn't feel any remorse. Maybe you're recovering without giving forgiveness a second thought. Whatever the reason, it's yours, and you have a right to it.

"Forgiveness fails as a reaction to severe, egregious and long-lasting harm because it does not reliably or necessarily help a harmed person regain trust simply by letting go of hostile feelings toward an offender. What the harmed person consistently experiences and that with which she must deal is harm itself and its attendant effects." ~ *Stanlick*

Today a reader named 'Bel' commented, "I gave myself closure about two months ago and my healing has now really escalated. After forgiving myself, all of the anger and pain dissipated – it comes back now and again – but with nowhere near the level and viciousness it hit me with for the best part of a year after separating. And I am better able to deal with it and let it go. Note: I have not forgiven him, I have forgiven myself. There is no obligation on our part to forgive someone who has deliberately gone out of their way to f**k us over, ever."

I could not agree more. Yet there is pressure to forgive, and if it doesn't come from others urging us to do so, it comes from ourselves, through the beliefs we've internalized that originate with our families, friends, religions, or cultures. But many believe the persistent myth that it is necessary, and then beat themselves up for not being able to forgive or for not wanting to forgive. After what these people have done — compounded by the fact that they have no remorse for it — do they deserve our forgiveness? We already gave them far more than enough forgiveness, again and again, and they kept blowing it.

I say own your feelings, because they exist for good reason. The day will come when you go on with your life and feel peaceful and happy, no forgiveness required.

"With respect to harm or wrongdoing, the traditional reactive attitudes and actions are forgiveness of, revenge against, and reconciliation with a perpetrator. Most accounts of forgiveness focus on benefits of forgiving to the forgiver and others. However, forgiveness, revenge, and traditional reconciliation may be impossible, inappropriate, or morally undesirable..." ~ *Stanlick*

As Solomon Schimmel notes, 'to advocate forgiving all offenders and all offenses because everyone commits some offenses blurs all distinction between degrees of sin, evil, and crime.' In short, Schimmel's view is that the simple fact that we all at some point commit some offense(s) does not lead to the conclusion that we are all equally culpable and thus equally forgivable since there are offenses that are significantly different in their effects or intentions from others that are minor, short-lived, or generally insignificant... Further, even if in general all of us commit some offense(s) at some time, this is largely irrelevant to specific cases in which the harmed person did not commit any offense against the offender."

Take the time to find what's right for you. There is no rush.

12 COMPASSION FOR THE PSYCHOPATH?

I imagine a day in the future when a cure for psychopathy is found.

Public announcements will be made informing psychopaths far and wide of free clinics that will offer the cure. An army of nurses in white will stand at the ready, their medicine cups arranged in neat and orderly rows, each holding one tiny blue pill. That sounds great, except for one thing...

Not one psychopath will show up.

Why would someone with a grandiose self-concept want a cure? A cure for *what?* Their superiority? Ask them and they'll tell you we're the ones who need a damned cure. They do not want to be like us. They feel contempt for us and believe we deserve to be abused.

Because of that, it is very difficult, if not impossible, to feel compassion for a psychopath.

I was inspired to write this article after someone said that although psychopaths aren't able to feel compassion, we are, and if that's true we need to have compassion for them. If we don't, she said, how are we any different?

Even if they are afflicted with a mental or neurobiological disorder, we are the ones who suffer because of it, not them. They experience contemptuous delight at the pain they inflict upon us. They choose who, when, and how they will abuse, so they do have some control over their behavior. They know right from wrong, but don't care. That does not inspire compassion.

It's hard to cue up the violins for people like that.

Yet most of us would welcome a cure for this disorder that condemns the afflicted to a life spent in a psychic landscape so alien to ours that psychopaths seem like...well, aliens. We welcome it because of what their disorder does to us. It wrecks their life too, but the thing is, they don't know it. They see it in a completely different way, and that makes it hard to feel any compassion for them.

Dr. Kent Kiehl, one of the world's leading investigators in psychopathy, has an interesting perspective on the problem. He says he is frustrated by the lack of respect shown to psychopathy by the mental-health establishment. 'Think about it. Crime is a trillion-dollar-a-year problem. The average psychopath (who has been convicted of a cime) will be convicted of four violent crimes by the age of forty. And yet hardly anyone is funding research into the science. Schizophrenia, which causes much less crime, has a hundred times more research money devoted to it."

Asked why, Kiehl said this:

'Because schizophrenics are seen as victims, and psychopaths are seen as predators. The former we feel empathy for, the latter we lock up.'

~ 'Suffering Souls,' The New Yorker

He makes a good point.

Kiehl is correct when he says more funding for research is needed. And part of it needs to go toward studying psychopaths who blend into society and ruin lives without ever seeing the inside of a jail cell. But good luck with that, since psychopathy isn't a even a diagnosis in the DSM, the 'bible' of psychiatry. How can something be funded if it doesn't exist?

You may be wondering why it's not a recognized diagnosis that can stand on its own, and why it is instead lumped in with antisocial personality disorder. Dr. Robert Hare considers that to be a mistake, and says this about it:

"Traditionally, affective (emotional) and interpersonal traits such as egocentricity, deceit, shallow affect, manipulativeness, selfishness, and lack of empathy, guilt or remorse, have played a central role in the conceptualization and diagnosis of psychopathy. In 1980 this tradition was broken...Psychopathy was re-named antisocial personality disorder and was now defined by persistent violations of social norms, including lying, stealing, truancy, inconsistent work behavior and traffic arrests.

Among the reasons given for this dramatic shift away from the use of clinical inferences were that personality traits are difficult to measure reliably, and that it is easier to agree on the behaviors that typify a disorder than on the reasons why they occur..."

~ Psychopathy and Antisocial Personality Disorder: A Case of Diagnostic Confusion, by Robert Hare, PhD.

In other words, the emotional and relational traits of psychopathy are too difficult to identify, so instead clinicians decided to look at behavioral traits because they're easier to see. Since criminal psychopaths have behavioral traits similar to those with ASPD, they stuck psychopathy in with that diagnosis. The pesky problem was solved! Or so it seemed to them.

To me, one of the main problems with that conclusion is this: *If you don't know the underlying cause of someone's behavior, how can you ever hope to change it?*

Another big problem is that the behavior of many psychopaths isn't so overtly antisocial that they end up in the legal system or in front of a clinician, so this stealth class of psychopaths isn't represented at all. These sub-criminal psychopaths are the type who victimized many of us. They committed moral crimes, and never ended up before a judge. They're largely a mystery to mental health professionals. As a result, that get away with their crimes against us without facing any consequences at all. They slip invisibly through the cracks that few even know exist.

In my research travels through cyberspace, I have repeatedly come upon an article in the search results titled 'The Hidden Suffering of the Psychopath." Every time I saw that title, I thought the psychiatrist who wrote it must have been duped. I didn't even want to look at it. When I finally did, I realized my hunch was correct. Everything he said went against all that is known about psychopathy.

Willem H.J. Martens, MD, PhD, says in the first paragraph, *"...Like healthy people, many psychopaths love their parents, spouse, children and pets in their own way."*

I took a deep breath, and continued reading.

"...Psychopaths can suffer emotional pain for a variety of reasons. Like anyone else, psychopaths have a deep wish to be loved and cared for."

Is that right?

Hmm...

I wondered where he got his information. I never heard anything like this before.

Martens went on to write, *"As psychopathic serial killers Jeffrey Dahmer and Dennis Nilson expressed, violent psychopaths ultimately reach a point of no return, where they feel they have cut through the last thin connection with the normal world. Subsequently their sadness and suffering increase..."*

As it turns out, the psychiatrist wrote his paper based on two serial killers, Dahmer and Nilson.

"...Dahmer and Nilsen have stated that they killed simply for company..."

They killed simply for *company?*

The problem is Dahmer and Nilson were never diagnosed as psychopathic. They both were diagnosed as schizoid, along with a dizzying array of other disorders (borderline, paranoid, etc.). It's not possible to come up with theories about psychopathy when you study subjects who aren't even psychopathic to begin with.

Martens writes, *"For the rest of us it is unimaginable that these men were so lonely — yet they describe their loneliness and social failures as unbearably painful."*

Psychopaths don't experience loneliness. I asked one if he did, and he had to look it up in the dictionary before he could answer my question. His answer was no. He said he felt boredom and had a great need for stimulation. His source of stimulation? People. Seeking out people because of a need for stimulation is different than seeking out people because of loneliness.

And seeking out people so you can kill them and prop them up in an easy chair in order to have 'company' is something else entirely.

Either Dahmer and Nilsen were psychopaths who duped this doctor and the ones who diagnosed them as schizoid, or they weren't psychopaths at all. What this doctor puts forth goes against all that is known about psychopathy. We know they have a very limited range of shallow emotions. If you believe what Martens writes, it will tug on your heart strings and quite possibly make you want to go back to that psychopath you knew and attempt to soothe his emotional agony. They don't have emotional agony, but they're very good at giving it to us.

Compassion for the psychopath? Better to have compassion for ourselves, because we are the ones who suffer as a result of their disorder.

13 FREEDOM: THE ULTIMATE RELATIONSHIP LITMUS TEST

The very first thing I felt after the psychopath discarded me was absolute and utter *relief.*

I remember the long, deep breath I took, and the feeling of my entire body relaxing. This feeling of relief was quickly overpowered by other emotions, but I will never forget that moment.

I was free again.

That means that I hadn't been free…and I didn't even realize it.

That's why Freedom will be the litmus test of all my future relationships.

I will ask myself:

Am I free from fear? Free from shame? Free from uncertainty? Free from feelings of inadequacy that I didn't have before? Am I free to express my emotions? Am I free to share my thoughts and opinions? *Am I free to be myself?*

Perhaps the loss of freedom is the biggest sign of involvement with a psychopath, or with any kind of abuser.

We couldn't see our loss of freedom at the time, but we can see it now, and we will be able to see it in the future.

When the 'relationship' began, we felt very free. We were loved and appreciated for who we were (or so we thought), so we were free to be ourselves. We took the risk to be vulnerable — one we were invited to take — but as we let ourselves be seen, something terrible began to happen. Instead of being accepted for who we were, inevitable flaws and all, we were Squashed. Crushed. Pummeled. Shamed. Silenced.

We began to hide ourselves out of fear of being rejected by our beloved. We hid our emotions, our intuitions and our doubts. Our joy at finding love turned into the fear of losing it (known as 'the manipulative shift'), and from that moment on we were imprisoned, slowly but surely, as our lover turned into our captor. We didn't see our prison cell being stealthily built, one bar at a time, as we lost our freedom bit by bit.

It's awful to go through the day motivated by the avoidance of rejection, hurt, and humiliation. It's like living in a pressure-cooker with the lid on tight. There is no freedom in living like that.

When it was over, we were safe and free to be ourselves — how wonderful! Except for one thing…

Our captivity didn't end when the relationship (victimization) ended.

We got stuck in a Betrayal Bond, an intense bond with the perpetrator that happens when an egregious betrayal of trust takes place. We were still not free. And we were at risk of reuniting with the abuser if he or she wanted to continue the abuse.

Shame and blame are large parts of a betrayal bond. Instead of clearly seeing what transpired, we blame ourselves and feel shame for what happened.

To become free, we must take the antidotes to the poison: No Contact. Learn the truth about psychopaths. Learn about betrayal bonds. Accept that we have been betrayed (and this is not easy —

betrayal, especially by the one we loved most, is shocking and devastating). Develop boundaries. Create healthy bonds with trustworthy friends, family members, a therapist, and a support group. Breaking a trauma bond is much different from "getting over someone." It takes understanding, work, determination, and self-compassion.

"In many ways, betrayal and exploitation are like being in the fun house. It makes the abnormal and the grotesque appear normal. Trauma distorts our perceptions just as sure as the mirrors in the fun house. Your task is to leave the fun house and face the reality without the distortion. This risk is the price of admission to recovery.

Saying good-bye is wrenching for survivors, who already grieve their many losses. Here the survivor must confront the deep desire for the seduction story to be true. There is more than exploitation or abuse at stake here. There is the loss of some dream or core hope that made the seduction story so irresistible. Usually that dream or hope has roots in some original wound for which the survivor has not yet fully grieved. So when it is time for good-bye, the grief will be overwhelming. The only choice you have to survive is to embrace the pain and experience the loss. In many ways the betrayal bond protected you against that pain…

You may not have to say good-bye, but you must be willing to do so. In fact, life as you know it may require a complete transformation for you to survive these relationships. Work, values, homes, friends, and even family relationships may have to substantively change for a successful recovery. What lengths are you willing to go to in order to be free? When you answer that question, you may have to face another risk; to be alone and be okay."

From 'The Betrayal Bond,' by Patrick Carnes, Ph.D

We forget that freedom is our right and our natural state, but when we get it back we remember. It feels good, and we will never give it up again.

14 In The Matrix of the Psychopath

The Matrix. It's one of my favorite movies ever. I got to thinking about how it parallels the experience with a psychopath when a reader named 'efemeris' said this:

"I connect psychopaths to computer hackers and viruses. They come in many forms and differ in the degree of their programmed function. What a virus, a spammer, a hacker or related threats do to a computer is what a psychopath does to us humans. And they will cover up their infection and act like 'normal' human beings in order to spread the infection."

Have you seen The Matrix? It's about a guy named Neo who believes he's living a normal but slightly empty and troubled life. By day, he's a computer programmer for a large software company. By night, he's a hacker. He lives alone, he barely sleeps, and there's a profound void in his life, but it's something he can't quite pinpoint – until he is contacted by a woman named Trinity. "It's the question that drives us," she whispers to him, to which he correctly responds "What is the Matrix?" This is the question that has gnawed away at Neo for years, yet he's never been able to put it into words until now. It is the voicing of this question that begins his transformation.

Neo learns he's not living in the real world at all — he only believes he is. In reality, he lives in a simulated world — and living a simulated life — that's been constructed for him.

The Matrix is an illusory world, one created to prevent humans from knowing they are slaves to an external influence.

55

The true nature of the Matrix is that it's a detailed computer simulation of life. It's been created to keep the minds of humans docile while their bodies are kept in pods stored in massive power plants, so their body heat and bioelectricity can be consumed as power by the sentient machines that have enslaved them.

The concept that the Matrix is a construct that humans are unaware of is similar to the idea of Samsara in Buddhism and Hinduism. Samsara teaches that the world we consider 'real' is actually a projection of our own desires.

How is this like the experience of involvement with a psychopath?

The psychopath came along and fulfilled our desires by creating an illusory world of love, in order to enslave us and feed on us. *We were existing in a matrix that the psychopath created. And we didn't know it.*

Neo learns that once he knows the truth, he will never be able to return to his old life.

Neo indicates his acceptance by choosing to swallow an offered red pill; his reality soon disintegrates and he abruptly wakes up, naked and wet, in a liquid-filled pod, finding himself as one of millions of people connected by cables to an elaborate electrical system, providing energy to those who enslaved them.

We had the same cold awakening when we realized the truth of what was happening to us, and we will never go back to our old lives, either.

The red pill and its opposite, the blue pill, are popular culture symbols. The red pill represents the painful truth of reality, while the blue pill represents the blissful ignorance of illusion. Neo swallows the red pill, which leads to his escape from the Matrix and into the real world, therefore living the "truth of reality," even though it is a harsh truth.

One of the characters Neo meets on his journey is called The Oracle. In Greek history, the oracle was an intermediary between God and man. People could ask an Oracle questions and get an answer, sometimes in a riddle format that often wouldn't make sense until later. In the Matrix, The Oracle cryptically says, "You know what that means? It's Latin. It means know thyself."

'Know thyself' is inscribed upon the Oracle of Apollo, and is attributed to the Delphic Oracle, of 6th century B.C. Greece.

Knowing ourselves better than we ever did before is one of the outcomes of our journey, too.

A central theme of the Matrix is Neo's heroic journey as the One. It's the hero's journey, one that every psychopath's victim is on (although it may go unrecognized).

Neo also meets a character known as "spoon boy." He has this conversation with him:

Spoon boy: *Do not try and bend the spoon. That's impossible. Instead only try to realize the truth.*

Neo: *What truth?*

Spoon boy: *There is no spoon.*

Neo: *There is no spoon?*

Spoon boy: *Then you'll see that it is not the spoon that bends, it is only yourself.*

The spoon exists only in the Matrix, which means it doesn't really exist at all. It's a lesson for Neo, to help him realize that manipulating the Matrix isn't about focusing on an object within it and trying to change it. The object doesn't exist, so he can't change it; he can only change himself, by becoming free.

Likewise, we can't change anything within the illusory world the psychopath created for us – the only thing we can do is free ourselves from it.

15 CAN WE EVER TRUST AGAIN?

"Don't ever trust anyone ever again!"

That was my mother's advice to me when I told her about the psychopath. My response was, "That would be a terrible life!"

As I imagined 'never trusting anyone again' because of what the psychopath had done, I had the mental image of being a suspicious, fearful person living an isolated life, one which was destroyed by him. I would be forever his victim, or at least until the day I died 'safe' and alone.

That would be a tragedy.

I had bigger plans for myself: I would learn from my experience, learn how to trust and who to trust, and develop confidence in myself.

The betrayal we experienced was devastating. After something like that, it's normal to withdraw and question everything and everyone. Our trust was violated, along with our hearts, our minds, and our souls. We close ourselves and turn inward. It is a necessary and beneficial part of the healing process.

"Who looks outside, dreams. Who looks inside, awakens."

~Carl Jung

But as humans, we have a drive to connect with others. At some point we will want to come out from our isolation. We will think about taking another risk.

"The risks of betrayal or rejection, though real, are outweighed by the certainty of insecurity and loneliness if we choose isolation."

~Gordon Shippey, Ph.D.

How do you know you're ready to trust again? What does it take to be ready?

It takes confidence. Not confidence in others, but confidence in yourself. Confidence in yourself means you trust yourself.

It's hard to trust others after what happened. It's also hard to trust ourselves. After all, we didn't see the truth of what was going on right before our eyes, and even if we did, the psychopath was good at filling us with self-doubt.

But we have learned a lot since then.

What is trust, exactly?

"Trust is the ability to be vulnerable with another person. When you trust someone, you feel certain this person will keep your best interests in mind. You believe they are who they say they are. You believe the deepest parts of you will be safe with them."

~ Townsend and Cloud, *Beyond Boundaries: Learning to Trust Again in Relationships*

A psychopath is an expert at gaining our trust. In the beginning they act like they're a trustworthy person, so we trust them. Then, as they change into an untrustworthy one, it's easy for them to pull it off. That's because once we have an image of someone as trustworthy in our minds, that image takes precedence over reality. It's simply a cognitive bias we all have, one of the many automatic ways in which our minds work.

Psychopaths know this, and they take full advantage of it. In the words of one anonymous psychopath,

"Trust is absolutely pivotal. I try to cultivate trust in any way I can. Empaths are blinded by positive emotions and are irrationally attached to the impressions they have of people. They are taught from an early age that there are 'good' people and there are 'bad' people. A solid sense of identity is extremely important to them, so everyone has to be categorized. Therefore, if someone thinks you are a 'good' person, you are automatically put into a box...So, how do you make people see you as a good person? That's where trust comes in. How do you build trust? In various ways. Random acts of kindness, understanding, and lavishing of attention, to name a few..."

Are we still just as vulnerable as we were before, or does awareness make a difference?

The psychopath goes on to say,

"Everyone around me is ranked based on usefulness, threat level and various other factors. As soon as someone's threat level usurps their usefulness level I dispose of them without fail."

And

"It is much more preferable to play with an unaware individual than an aware one."

We are aware now. That makes us much less preferable. It might even make us a threat.

Who should we trust?

Trustworthy people are those who habitually do the things that engender trust. They keep their word. Their actions and words match. They aren't deceitful. They don't arouse suspicion. They don't violate the boundaries they know we have. And they behave this way consistently over the course of a relationship. Trust can only be built over time.

"Trustworthiness is an abiding character state. A trustworthy person is someone who is reliable, consistent, and truthful in his or her actions across the board. It isn't that this person is perfect. Rather, her actions tend to spring from and reinforce her moral values and commitments." ~ Peg O'Connor, Ph.D.

A person who is worthy of your trust isn't just trustworthy sometimes…they're trustworthy all the time. On an ongoing basis.

Psychopaths can't do that because they're not really trustworthy at all — they only pretend to be, but their charade fails again and again because no one can keep up an act all the time, as the anonymous psychopath tells us:

"I can't imagine even the most skilled manipulator can pretend to be human 24/7."

Instead of losing self-confidence because of what happened, you can actually end up having more than ever before. 'Failure' can build our confidence because of what it can teach us, if only we are willing to learn and to believe in our knowledge, our experience, and ourselves.

Having confidence in yourself means that you trust yourself.

"The person you need to trust first is yourself. No one can be as consistently supportive of you as you can learn to be. Being kind to yourself increases self-confidence and lessens your need for approval. Loving and caring for yourself not only increases self-trust, it also deepens your connection with others." ~ Cynthia Wall, LCSW

A bird sitting on a branch is never afraid of the branch breaking, because her trust is not in the branch, but in her own wings.

Other components of self-trust include being aware of your thoughts and feelings and expressing them, following your personal standards and ethical code (in other words, sticking to your boundaries), knowing when you need to care for yourself first, and knowing you can survive mistakes.

Self-confidence is the state of self-assuredness and trust in yourself and your strengths and abilities. After our experience with a psychopath we are much more skilled at assessing people's behavior, and using those our observations to determine their character. Actions speak louder than words, and observing someone over time and in different situations can show us what kind of person they are.

Psychopaths are always putting on an act, and they don't want to be caught:

"When your whole life -- the very fabric of your being -- is a lie, you have much to be suspicious of. Every prolonged look is a highly trained P.I., every snapped twig a psychiatrist with straight jacket in tow."

Now we have a greater chance of being that detective who can identify who they are beneath the surface, that 'psychiatrist' who can astutely listen and observe and discern the truth.

~

"Damned empaths and their fairy tales — makes them too knowledgeable about villains, apparently."

Damned psychopaths and their fairy tales — makes us too knowledgeable about villains, apparently.

SECTION TWO: THE PSYCHOPATH

16 THE PSYCHOPATH: TRULY AND FUNDAMENTALLY DIFFERENT

"My mother, the most beautiful person in the world. She was strong, she worked hard to take care of four kids. A beautiful person. I started stealing her jewelry when I was in the fifth grade. You know, I never really knew the bitch — we went our separate ways."

From *Without Conscience,* Dr. Robert Hare

Despite what is known about psychopaths — they have no conscience, they're human predators, they have no real identity, they wear masks to blend in, they purposely manipulate and harm others — many people still hold tight to their mistaken beliefs that psychopaths are 'acting out their issues.' They believe psychopaths act as they do because of deep wounds to their psyches or a failure to bond with their mothers.

Some people are simply unable to grasp that another human could be so drastically different from themselves, as evidenced by comments like this one that I received from a reader:

"...And you know what? I am sure the psychopath isn't even aware of this destruction...he is a big, big, helpless child, seeking for attention and life-connections..."

I'm not just speaking about victims who don't understand. Many mental health professionals don't get it either, because they're hopelessly stuck within traditional psychological paradigms. This is a real tragedy because victims can get no help from such therapists, and in fact will suffer more harm at their hands.

66

"We've all heard the explanations: People abuse because they were abused themselves and act out their inner pain; Bullies are really cowards 'underneath;' Those who try to assert power and control over others are really insecure individuals, suffering from low-self esteem; Serial cheaters have trust wounds and are therefore 'commitment-phobic,' etc. And even though great strides have been made in recent years with respect to recognizing the true nature of character disturbance, some of these notions, derived from traditional psychology paradigms, unfortunately persist despite mounds of empirical evidence that they are in error."

~ George Simon, PhD, expert on manipulators and other problem characters, author of In Sheep's Clothing: Understanding and Dealing with Manipulative People. Quote from his article, 'Serious Abusers And Psychology's Failure to Understand Them'

Even when psychopaths themselves tell us how their minds work, it is hard for some to accept as the truth:

"Tony then explained how 'fucking stupid' most people are and believe anything as long as you liberally apply the words 'I Love you'. He then said, "The best ones are the ones who didn't get any love as kids; parents were a bit cold and so on. People from these families will do anything if you tell them you love them. They are like addicts or something. They never had, you know, parental affection and love as kids. It's a bit weird, alright, but you can spot these a mile away." ~Defeated Demons: Freedom from Consciousness Parasites in Psychopathic Society, by Thomas Sheridan

"When I look for these people, I look for someone to exploit, someone to expose all their weaknesses to themselves and leave them broken, hating themselves more than most of them already do. I enjoy causing people to realize the nasty truths of themselves (which is usually that they are pathetic lying individuals) even if I have to be hypocritical and lie myself in order to get my point across." ~ a female psychopath

Here are words from James Fallon, PhD, a psychopathic person, explaining how he interacts with his wife, sister and mother:

"...I don't treat them all that well... I treat my family...like they're just somebody at a bar... It's a kind of cruelty, a kind of abuse...You don't want to be married to me or be my kid or close friend because I'll kind of dump you, and I don't even think about it."

Simon neatly sums up the truth about psychopaths here:

"Psychopaths are the only known intra-species predators. And, as I assert in my writings and have learned from years of experience with such folks, the reason for this is that they consider themselves superior creatures compared to common humans. They have the most malignant form of narcissism. They know all too well how different they are from the rest of us but don't consider this a shortcoming. Rather, they consider themselves more than 'special.' They consider themselves distinctly superior to those who possess two characteristics they don't have: empathy and conscience. The way they see it, folks with a heart and with those things the rest of us call 'qualms' are an inferior breed, the perfect patsies, and their rightful prey."

Still don't quite grasp it? That's OK, because the truth is so difficult to understand from our own point of view. But when you do get it, it will go far in helping you to heal.

17 NARCISSIST OR PSYCHOPATH?

It's hard to tell the difference. Both are self-absorbed, arrogant and insensitive. They share similar characteristics and behaviors, and both are incredibly destructive to those unfortunate enough to become victims. But underneath these similarities, they are distinctly dissimilar. Their thought processes, motivations, and intentions are as different as night and day.

Narcissists and psychopaths are egocentric and focus on their own needs and desires. Both demand and feel entitled to gratification, and see others as existing to fulfill their needs. Both devalue and abuse others. But that's where the similarity ends and each takes a different path into a neural twilight zone.

Narcissists

Although it's commonly believed that narcissists are in love with themselves, the truth is they have deep feelings of inadequacy. Acknowledging that would be too painful, so they cultivate the delusion that they're perfect and wonderful and try to get others to reflect this back to them. Narcissists can only see themselves as they are reflected by others, so projecting a 'perfect' image becomes everything. They create a grandiose pseudo-persona — a parody of themselves — and cling to it for dear life. The reactions of others determine the value of this persona, and therefore their level of self-worth.

They seek attention, validation, adoration, and envy because they desperately *need* them in order to feel loved, adequate, and important.

If the narcissist doesn't get these things, his ego is punctured and his self-esteem deflates like a leaky hot-air balloon.

Narcissists are very concerned with what others think of them because they need admiration like others need oxygen. It is their 'supply,' the substance that feeds them.

Because of this, they are very vulnerable to being rejected, humiliated, upstaged, ignored, and going unrecognized for how special they are. When any of these things happen, they are deeply wounded and rage results. This rage — resulting from the 'narcissistic injury' — is expressed as passive-aggression or outright aggression.

Psychopaths

In contrast, psychopaths think very highly of themselves. In fact, they believe they're far superior to everyone else. They're supremely confident and have a grandiose sense of self-worth. They do not need attention or acceptance, except as a means to an end. When a psychopath is ignored or rejected, they don't care — their self-esteem has nothing to do with what others think of them. What they will experience is frustration, because psychopaths need to gain the attention and admiration of others in order to lure them as potential victims so they can satisfy their needs.

Psychopaths have no identity and they create pseudo-personas (masks) as needed, each tailor-made for an intended target of manipulation. Unlike the narcissist, the psychopath has no attachment to these personas. They're merely disguises that enable them to get what they want.

Psychopaths are predators on a perpetual hunt for superficial self-gratification. They have no emotional dependence on being noticed or admired like the narcissist does. Capturing the attention of another is simply the first step to gaining power and control.

"Both the psychopath and the narcissist disregard society, its conventions, social cues and social treaties.

But the psychopath carries this disdain to the extreme and is likely to be scheming, calculated, ruthless, and callous…Psychopaths are deliberately and gleefully evil while narcissists are absent-mindedly and incidentally evil."

- Sam Vaknin, psychopath

To compare and contrast the narcissist and psychopath, let's use the example of compulsive sexual infidelity (which is very common for both):

Both narcissists and psychopaths lie easily and persuasively. When their partner approaches them with suspicions, both will act outraged that they could ever have such doubts about them. The partner will feel guilty and shamed.

So far, the narcissist and the psychopath seem very similar. But when you look beneath the surface of their behavior, there are profound differences.

Narcissists cheat because they are deeply insecure and need validation to reassure them that they're still sexually attractive. If they aren't repeatedly reassured in this manner their self-esteem crumbles, they feel worthless, and they fall into despair.

Narcissists have a conscience, so they must rationalize their bad behavior in order to be able to continue to seek the validation they need. They do this by mentally blaming their partners for not appreciating them enough, therefore making the infidelity their partner's fault. After cheating, the narcissist feels reassured that he's still attractive, and his ego has been re-inflated. When it begins to deflate once again, he'll repeat the process in order to pump himself back up.

In contrast, psychopaths cheat because life is a game that has no rules, so they simply do whatever they want just because they feel like it. Psychopaths have no conscience, so they have no need for rationalizations. After cheating, the psychopath feels amused because he once again manipulated someone into having sex with him.

To sum it up:

Narcissists seek attention from others for its own sake, and they're emotionally wounded if they're rejected.

Psychopaths seek attention from others as a method to get something else, so they do not feel any emotional pain if they're rejected, although they will feel frustration at not getting what they want.

18 PSYCHOPATHS ARE NOT SUPERNATURAL BEINGS WITH SUPERPOWERS

A unsettling theme appears in some of the comments I get from readers on my website. I hear from people regularly who tell me there is no way they will ever be able to protect themselves from another psychopathic victimization. They feel powerless and hopeless, at the mercy of fate or luck or the benevolence of those with whom they cross paths. After all, they say, psychopaths are so powerful, so crafty, so...Not Really Human. This belief is dangerous because when you imbue them with other-worldly power, you are saying that you are powerless against such a force.

In the acute aftermath of my involvement with a psychopath, it seemed to me I had been involved with a Magician, or something of a different species entirely. How else could he have done what he did? It was totally out of left field, something I could never have anticipated or prevented because I never even knew it existed. I was blindsided, tricked, manipulated, disassembled, and left in pieces. I visited the victim forums online looking for support, validation and an explanation, and many times I saw psychopaths referred to as Evil or as Aliens or The Devil or some other sort of Supernatural Being who was Armed with Superpowers that Mere Humans are Powerless Against. I was traumatized and bewildered and in light of what I'd experienced, it seemed to me this could very well be true. Many of you who have experienced a psychopath understand what I'm saying. It was just that bad, just that breathtakingly unfathomable and incomprehensible.

But as time went on and I learned about psychopaths and how they work, I stripped them of their supernatural status. Is their behavior evil? Yes, but they are not evil beings unleashed from the depths of hell. Are they so different that they seem like aliens? Sure, but they are not actually aliens. Are they so skilled at manipulation that they seem like magicians? Certainly, but they are not really Merlin, complete with a wizard's hat and a magic wand. To give them such status makes them omnipotent…and it leaves us powerless in comparison.

Mary Ellen O'Toole, PhD., forensic psychologist, senior FBI profiler, and psychopathy expert, says "Using the term 'monster' throws us back to the 18th century when werewolves and vampires were blamed for violent crimes. We've come a long way since then and we know so much more about criminal behavior. Similarly, 'Evil' has no legal or behavioral meaning. It implies demonic possession…Understanding what they are will help you to understand their behavior. Thinking of Ariel Castro (who kidnapped three young women and held them prisoner for eleven years) as an evil monster may make us feel better, but it does nothing to further our understanding of what happened and maybe how to prevent it in the future. Words matter and labels make a difference."

Consider this: Psychopaths look at us with disgust for falling for their tricks, games and manipulations. Doesn't that say they don't really think they're so amazingly clever and powerful? So why should we think they are? We're on to them now, and that's worth a lot more than we might believe, if only we'd believe it.

So if psychopaths aren't supernatural beings with amazing superpowers, why do some of us believe that they are?

According to Sartre, magic is dominant when control over our experience is weak:

"Magical beliefs and the fearful reactions based on such beliefs are the result of the state of uncertainty we are in, created by this challenge and by the negation of our expectations. Our feelings come from the conviction of loss of control and the sense of helplessness we feel when our cognitive system can neither assimilate our experience into its own structure nor adapt itself to the structure of the experience."

Remember the All-Powerful Wizard of Oz and how he turned out to be the mere mortal trickster hiding behind the curtain? It's a bit like that. I'm not saying a psychopath is actually like the loveable, bumbling old guy the wizard turned out to be. What I'm saying is that when you divest the psychopath of his or her above-human supernatural status by learning how he or she really operates, you'll bring him down several notches to a level you will find more manageable, one that leaves you feeling you're not completely without power.

This doesn't mean you won't be at risk, and it's not meant to make you over-confident, which could potentially put you at even more risk. It is simply to see them for what they really are, to de-mystify them, and to recognize that what you've experienced, and all you've learned about them since then, and what you've done to shore up your defenses (like developing boundaries and knowing your vulnerabilities), can help protect you from future victimization.

Current research says that psychopaths are born neurologically different. This may or may not combine with the environment they're raised in to determine the final outcome. One prominent theory says that in a psychopath's brain the amygdala is not connected to the pre-frontal cortex, meaning the emotions are not connected to the decision-making processes or other executive functions.

This neurological difference is obviously very significant (especially to those of us who have experienced it). It leaves a person without a conscience, without most emotions, and without the ability to feel love or experience remorse. It creates a callous and coldly analytical person whose thoughts and actions are instrumental, self-serving and only to reach some goal (summed up as: predatory). I once read psychopaths described as "effectively intelligent rational agents." I think that fits.

Bereft of the usual human drives to bond with others, experience love, or create close relationships — yet still in possession of an intelligent, curious mind and plenty of energy — they're driven to do something. There are a lot of hours to fill in a day! So they will do what they're capable of doing and what is within their nature to do, and some of that is to manipulate and use others for personal gain or stimulation. Do they hurt everyone they come into contact with? No. They understand the value of having allies and in developing connections that can help them in some way. They do know right from wrong, and they pick and choose who will be on the receiving end of that wrong. While these are all very significant, they're not superhuman or supernatural.

In your recovery, you'll get to the point where the psychopathic bond is finally broken (yes, it will happen) and your future lies in front of you. Will you go forth in fear or with confidence? One way you can go on with confidence is to ditch the belief that psychopaths are some sort of inexplicable, inhuman beings that you are powerless against.

Believing that will do nothing to help you, and it will definitely hinder you.

19 SHINY OBJECTS: A DEEPER LOOK AT IDEALIZATION AND DEVALUATION

When a shiny object captures a psychopath's attention, watch out.

They are intensely goal-driven, and their attention is as narrow and focused as a laser beam. When they see something they want they will do whatever it takes to get it.

Psychopaths actually see people around them as objects, so this is not simply a metaphor or an analogy. And they have a desire to possess the object that sparkles and shines and catches their eye. When you are that shiny object, you are in serious trouble. Unbeknownst to you, you are commandeered to play a part in a cycle the psychopath must repeat in order to remain intact.

When a psychopath sets his sights on you — the shiny new thing he becomes fascinated with – he idealizes you, just as someone would after seeing a shiny new car in a showroom window. At that point, he will see you as nearly flawless. Of course no one is flawless, especially to a psychopath. But somehow, he may believe you are if he is idealizing you.

Inevitably, he will be disappointed.

As the psychopath gets to know you he starts seeing what he considers weaknesses. To a psychopath, weaknesses are contemptible. His inherently fragile image of you as a flawless object cracks and shatters, and he sees the horrifying truth – you are only human. The shiny object isn't shiny anymore. He is disgusted and he loses interest. That's when devaluation begins.

He now sees you as pathetic. He may stick around for a while since he's getting some need fulfilled – sex, money, maintaining the illusion of a marriage, or something else — but while he's fulfilling that need, he will manipulate and abuse you, believing you deserve it. And he will enjoy doing it because it gives him a feeling of contemptuous delight.

For a psychopath, to know you is to hate you. You didn't really do anything wrong (although he wants you to believe you did). Likewise, you weren't idealized for anything you truly were, only for what the psychopath imagined you to be. But you are a real person, not a product of the psychopath's imagination. The psychopath is not capable of understanding that.

In a normal relationship, as we get to know someone we learn each other's vulnerabilities and accept each other's flaws. That's precisely what creates emotional intimacy. But with a psychopath, it's the exact opposite. And many of the things they see as flaws are just normal human behavior. In fact, many of these things are our strengths. But in the psychopath's world, things are topsy-turvy. The psychopath sees our strengths as flaws, and sees his flaws as strengths. They think things like love, trust, and compassion make us fools who are easy to manipulate, while they think their ability to lie, manipulate, and act without remorse makes them strong and superior.

A psychopath who read some things I've posted on this site thought much of it was 'spot-on'…except for one thing. He repeatedly took issue with my claim that a psychopath's goal, from day one, is to cause harm. He said this wasn't *always* the case. He said that although he was incapable of falling in love, he did sometimes become fascinated with someone. And he said that every time he did, he quickly lost his infatuation because the person 'blew it.' When they did, he thought they were pathetic. After that, he would become abusive.

I didn't believe him when he said he sometimes became fascinated with someone. I stuck to my claim that it was all about harm from the beginning. But with further reading and learning, I found out he may have been truthful.

Even if they do start out as 'fascinated' harm is inevitable, so this discovery doesn't change things in any consequential way. Idealization (fascination) is not love, and it will always turn into devaluation, which always causes harm.

But the reason behind it, if true, is damn interesting.

According to Dr. Reid J. Meloy in 'The Psychopathic Mind: Origins, Dynamics, and Treatment' – a challenging book that an integrates the biological and psychodynamic understanding of psychopathy, and is considered the definitive book on the subject — devaluing someone enhances the psychopath's grandiosity and sense of superiority. He experiences exhilaration and contempt ('contemptuous delight'). Devaluation is driven by unconscious greed and envy. The psychopath's hatred creates wishes to destroy the object, which in turn eliminates his envy.

It is important to understand that envy is hatred of the good object, and greed is the desire to have all the 'contents' of the good object (and now I might know why the psychopath I knew told me he was a vampire).

"What he gets he spoils and wastes; he feels frustrated and deprived, and the greed and demand start again."

Devaluation is a form of 'splitting' (seeing things as all good or all bad) that empties the psychopath's world of people and values.

Psychopaths experience a "zero state," an inner feeling an emptiness, which is the closest they will ever get to depression, according to Meloy. Yet devaluation perpetuates these feelings of emptiness by warding off any object that would empathize with the psychopath's plight.

So why must the psychopath continue to devalue? Meloy says the psychopath must act out this manipulative cycle repetitively and compulsively in order to experience feelings of exhilaration and contempt, which perpetuate his feeling of grandiosity. If the psychopath were to inhibit this behavior, for whatever reason, it would cause conscious envy and rage, and lower the psychopathic threshold for violence. The manipulative cycle is a 'purification process' for the psychopath, which projects all the bad onto the victim of his manipulation. It is described as a narcissistic repair of the psychopathic process that restores a primitive and defensive equilibrium. They need to do this because their grandiose self is threatened with intrapsychic rupture, but must be kept intact.

The psychopath will continue to ward off others by devaluing them, Meloy says, but also continue to seek out new victims. Once he finds a victim his greed and envy cause rage and sadism, and the victim is devalued and destroyed. When that is accomplished, the cycle starts all over again. They move on to the next shiny object that captures their attention and repeat this never-ending cycle.

Ultimately, what motivates the psychopath isn't of any real importance to victims. Whatever their motivation, their behavior it always results in serious harm. I simply offer this as an interesting theory.

20 PSYCHOPATHIC SEDUCTION SECRETS, REVEALED!

What makes psychopaths such legendary seducers?

Why did Don Juan get all the girls?

Finally, here they are...

Seduction Secrets of the Psychopath!

Psychopaths have a grandiose, unshakeable, pathological sense of self-confidence.

They feel no fear, so they have no social anxiety. They can approach anyone without becoming nervous.

They're pathological liars who will say anything to get what they want. They have no integrity, so honesty means nothing to them

They're predators, so they focus on their target like a laser beam. It's the focus of a predator on his prey, adorned with a smile. Literally.

That intense focus allows them to be totally present, which feels so very pleasing to the target.

They have no identity, so they can be whomever their target needs them to be. They put on personas the way others put on a pair of pants.

They're astute psychologists with the ability to clearly and easily see someone's vulnerabilities.

Manipulation comes naturally, so they know just how to exploit those vulnerabilities.

They also manipulate so well because they have no other way of dealing with people and no other reason for dealing with them.

They have no conscience, so they don't feel bad about anything they do. They have no problem looking themselves in the eye after manipulating, using and damaging someone.

They have no morals. They know the difference between right and wrong, but they just don't care.

They have no ability to love, but they have the ability to act as if they do.

They don't honor commitments, but they don't hesitate to make them anyway if it gets them what they want.

They take no responsibility for themselves or for others.

They become bored quickly, which drives them to move from one ~~lover~~ victim to the next to the next.

Their lives are an empty and meaningless game, so they have nothing better to do.

Oh, I forgot one...

Psychopaths are so charming. *Aren't they?*

21 What Ebola Can Teach Us About Psychopaths

I wanted to write about those suffering with the Ebola virus and the very brave people who help them. But this book is about psychopaths, so I needed to find a way to connect them. I found my answer when I went to the website of Doctors Without Borders. DWB has been fighting the epidemic tirelessly in West Africa. They posed this challenge on their site:

"A Day Without Touch is a solidarity challenge and fundraiser that raises awareness of the way Ebola 'parasitizes' humanity, using our most human impulses — to touch and care for those who are sick and in need — to propagate disease."

"...Ebola parasitizes humanity..."

Indeed it does. Psychopaths parasitize humanity, too. I found the connection I needed.

Ebola is a horrific disease that kills 50 – 70 percent of its victims in an especially terrible way. But there is something else at work that is just as horrifying as the disease itself. Unlike diseases that infect people by spreading through the air, Ebola infects through close contact.

In other words, Ebola infects through love, by way of infecting those who care for the sick.

"This virus preys on care and love, piggybacking on the deepest, most distinctively human virtues."

~ Benjamin Hale, 'The Most Terrifying Thing About Ebola'

Psychopaths prey on their victims in the very same way.

A psychopath who wishes to ensnare us in a false relationship first needs to draw us close enough to be victimized. They do this by manipulating us into loving them. Our ability to love is what enables the psychopath to infect our lives, our hearts and our souls.

Direct contact with body fluids is the primary way Ebola spreads. What's startling is that the virus itself *causes* the production of massive amounts of body fluids so that it can perpetuate itself. It purposely causes victims to projectile vomit and have massive diarrhea, and to bleed from their eyes, ears, and gastrointestinal tract. When others care for them, these fluids infect them.

Viruses are intelligent in that way – *they program their host to behave in a manner that ensures their goal is met,* which is to infect others so the virus itself can stay alive. Rabies is another good example. It is spread through saliva, and what better way is there to get saliva into the skin than to cause the infected host to become vicious and bite?

Hale writes,

"Every mechanism we have for caring—touching, holding, feeding, playing, warming, comforting, caressing — every mechanism that we use to bind us to our families and our neighbors, is preyed upon by Ebola...We are humans, and we will care about our children and our families even if it means that we may die in doing so."

Even when things started going terribly wrong in our relationship – which, unknown to us, was with a psychopath – we were programmed to continue. We were unable to see the truth of what was happening because of their manipulation and because of our humanity -- we saw the psychopath as someone who was loving and trustworthy and who had our best interests at heart. The psychopath presented themselves to us in that way, and our human nature didn't allow us to see them any differently, at least not for a while.

Psychopaths know this all too well, and it's what makes their manipulation possible. They infect us by pretending to love us, and then when the incubation (idealization) period is over, the symptoms of infection (devaluation) start to emerge.

We start to realize that something strange is happening beneath the surface, but we can't pull back. *Love keeps us in the hot zone.* The same thing happens with the caregivers of those with Ebola. Love will not allow them to step away and save themselves.

"The lesson here is a vital one: People do not give up on humanity so very easily. Even if we persuade all of the population to forgo rituals like washing the dead, we will not easily persuade parents to keep from holding their sick children, and children from clinging to their ailing parents…The love and compassion that puts people at risk of infection will not stop in the Ebola zone. Humans can't give them up, because it is fundamental to what we are," Hale wrote.

'People do not give up on humanity so very easily.' How true.

"The problem is double-edged. Ebola threatens humanity by preying on humanity. The seemingly simple solution is to destroy humanity in ourselves…but doing so means destroying ourselves in order to save ourselves, which is no solution at all."

The problem is the same when considering psychopaths. They threaten our humanity by preying on our humanity. If we destroy the humanity in ourselves, a psychopath who attempted to victimize us wouldn't have a chance. But doing so means destroying ourselves in order to keep ourselves safe, which is no solution at all. We would end up just like them, and life would be a meaningless void.

"The only one way to battle a disease that affixes itself parasitically to our humanity is to overwhelm it with greater, stronger humanity. To immunize

89

Africa and the rest of the world with a blast of humanity so powerful that the disease can no longer take root."

Likewise, we can immunize ourselves and each other from psychopaths with a blast of humanity. Help from others may be lacking because they are unable to understand, so this blast of humanity must come from us, in the form of support, validation, encouragement, and information.

"If we seek safety by shutting out the rest of the world, we are in for a brutally ugly awakening. Nature is a cruel mistress, but Ebola is her cruelest, most devious trick yet."

Ebola…and psychopaths.

Psychopathy is a cruel trick to us, and also to psychopaths themselves — although they will never be able to understand that.

22 Hocus-Pocus: It's All In the Focus

"You were so vulnerable — that's why I chose you, and why I was able to bond with you so quickly and so deeply."

The psychopath I was involved with spoke these words to me the last time I saw him. It sickened me to hear them and to learn that my suspicions about him were correct. He wasn't even trying to hide the truth any longer. He may as well have just come right out and said "I'm a psychopath." So what did I do next? Did I storm off, or yell at him about what a creep he was, or tell him to get lost?

Nope.

Just a few moments later, I was dancing and laughing in his arms, having a great time as usual, as if it had never happened. Somehow, I'd forgotten what he said just a few moments earlier. I had no memory of his words until the next morning.

When I remembered, I was shocked. How was it possible I could forget something like that, I wondered?

In fact, each time I saw him I forgot all the doubts I had and all the lies he told me.

I found the answer a couple of months later, and then it made sense (along with everything else).

Psychopaths are natural hypnotists.

They don't need to swing a gold watch back and forth, because they have one built in. It comes naturally to them because of what they are. Because they're predators, they focus on us like a laser beam, completely without distraction. Nothing gets between them and their target. Because of this focus they're completely and totally present, on a level that probably puts the Dali Lama to shame.

We spend a lot of time lost in our own heads. We're lost in thought, lost in worries about the future or regrets about the past, or preoccupied with some crisis in our lives.

The psychopath, however, is never lost in his head.

In fact, he's not in his head at all — he's in yours.

A psychopath lives squarely in the present moment and experiences reality like the clear, cold light of a cloudless winter day.

When we're the focus of the psychopath's intense presence, we don't notice it for what it really is. We just notice that this person is very interested in us, so we become interested in them. It feels wonderful to be so captivating. We've finally met someone who really appreciates us and who is deeply interested in us. On a subconscious level, it feels good — amazingly good — to be the focus of this presence. We become completely absorbed in it. Our own focus narrows, and we become oblivious to the world around us. Our sense of time is altered — minutes seem like hours or hours seem like minutes. The frequency of our brain waves slows in response to the changed level of mental activity. *We are in a trance.*

The problem (beside the psychopath) is that we mistake the psychopath's predatory focus for the focus of someone who is enamored with us. After all, they don't look like or act predators. They smile and say all the right things. If we only knew what they were really thinking…

Trance states are highly pleasing to both the conscious and subconscious mind. It's an altered mental state, like the high experienced from a potent drug. We seek it. We even become addicted to it. Not only does it feel good; wonderful things happen when we're in our psychopath-induced trance. Everything good we experience in the relationship happens within this state of mind. These moments are bathed in oxytocin and dopamine, powerful brain chemicals that make us feel connected and euphoric and keep us coming back for another fix.

Naturally, we want to return to such a pleasant state over and over again, and the psychopath is glad to help us get there — non-stop in the beginning, but less and less as time goes on. With this positive reinforcement in the beginning to get us hooked — and then intermittent reinforcement to *keep* us hooked — it's a hopeless situation. We don't realize any of this consciously while it's happening. Even years later, we miss those magical moments that seemed to sparkle with fairy dust and glow with a warm ethereal light. It seemed too perfect for this world, but we were happy that it was ours nonetheless.

The intense bond that forms between a victim and a psychopath at the beginning of the relationship is due in part to the "hypno-powers" of the psychopath, according to Sandra L. Brown, M.A., author of *Women Who Love Psychopaths*. In fact, she says hypnosis and trance are the "attraction heat, attachment magnet and bonding glue" of the relationship.

It's also what keeps us coming back for more when things are falling apart.

An excerpt from H.G. Beverly, author of *The Other Side of Charm: Your Memoir*:

"You will fall in love. Your love will come to you from the southeast in some kind of subtle-sparkle-smoke fog coming in through the cracks around your door sweeping across the room to you there where you'll be reading on your sofa he'll be reaching his hands down around your waist filling your eyes with his glow so intense that you will not keep yourself from looking over and away.....You won't have known what it could be what might happen in your heart when the sparks start flying to the sky when the light show creates a fog and you won't have known what love could feel like to be lost what the smoke might do to your heart all engulfed in that glittering, hazy mist no time to come up for air you won't even bother trying. You won't have known what it could be until it finds its way in through the cracks and then you'll know that nothing was like this before so this is the one there's no way of saying no when God sends you the smoke you don't question your destiny.

You won't question your destiny."

23 SPACESHIP MOMENTS

When the psychopath came to see me he parked his spaceship just around the corner, out of my line of sight.

He must have.

There were so many strange things he said. Out of place. Out of context. *Out of the blue.* Like an alien being who didn't get humans or life on earth at all, but who was trying to understand. On an intellectual level, he knew enough to use it for personal gain. But deep down, he didn't get it...

...because there was no deep down.

I now know that the bizarre things he said were big clues to his true nature.

Instead of questioning him or running screaming from the room, I made a joke out of it. Or I patiently answered his questions, as if I were talking to a child or a tourist from the Orion galaxy. Or I saw him as a sensitive man who was trying to understand me and himself and love and this crazy, crazy world. Or something.

But I should have run screaming from the room, because the man was telling me he was a psychopath.

Last year I read an article titled "10 Signs Your Man Is A Psychopath," and it said this:

"A psychopath will sometimes blurt out something odd about himself, apropos of nothing. Like you might be cooking dinner and suddenly he blurts, 'I'm crazy you know.'"

I'd heard plenty of things like that. I had come to think of them as "Spaceship Moments." Here are just a few of them. He said each one without the slightest hint of humor.

Psychopath: "Why do we have sex?"

Me: The way he asked caused me to reply, "Do you mean you and I...or the entire human race?"

P: He shrugged his shoulders and said, "I dunno — Anybody!"

P: "What's the difference between being in love and loving someone?"

Me: "You can love your mother or your brother, but you're not in love with them, right? When you're in love, it's romantic love."

P: Looked dumfounded and said, "That's bullshit! Really?"

P: "I'm a pervert, you know."

Me: "What? You're the least perverted person I've ever known!"

P: *"I'm a pervert."*

P: "We sure do get along great for two strangers, don't we?"

Me: Struck speechless.

P: "I'm a vampire."

Me: "You can't be — the sun is shining!"

P: "No, really — I'm a vampire."

P: "I've never been depressed in my life. I can't even understand it."

P: "I've never felt stressed, ever. I don't understand this 'stress' thing at all."

P: I'm not afraid of anything. I can't really say that I've ever felt fear."

I understand these things now, and even get a laugh thinking of a couple of them.

But there is one thing he said, several times, out of the blue, that I will never, ever laugh about, and it is this:

"Some people aren't capable of love, you know."

It never crossed my mind that he was talking about himself.

~

Many victims report hearing similar types of things. When someone says strange things like this, don't just brush it off, find some explanation, or think it's endearing. See it for the warning that it is.

24 WALKING THROUGH THE SHADOW OF THE UNCANNY VALLEY

The psychopath I was involved with sometimes made strange and disturbing facial expressions.

A sad face with the corners of his mouth turned up just a little too much. A high-voltage smile that would have blown every transformer in town if he were hooked up to the grid. A Heath-Ledger-Joker-Face I caught twice when I turned around quickly, which came across as a sinister duping hysteria. And a face that was so devoid of expression that he looked just like a corpse — slack, gray, and emotionless, punctuated by two lifeless eyes.

These faces struck me as being uncanny. The first two came across as not-quite-right, and the last two came across as downright disturbing.

What exactly does uncanny mean?

"The uncanny ('the opposite of what is familiar') is a Freudian concept of an instance where something can be both familiar yet alien at the same time, resulting in a feeling of it being uncomfortably strange. Because the uncanny is familiar, yet incongruous, it often creates cognitive dissonance within the experiencing subject, due to the paradoxical nature of being simultaneously attracted to yet repulsed by an object."

~Wikipedia

Because the psychopath wears a mask to hide himself, there are two kinds of facial expressions we may see:

Those that are meant to convey some type of emotion he's not really feeling, and those that are his real expressions, the ones he tries to suppress.

When we see these facial expressions and recognize them as a little bit 'off,' downright fake, or just plain strange as hell, we are experiencing 'the uncanny valley.'

What is the uncanny valley?

"The uncanny valley is a hypothesis in the field of human aesthetics which holds that when human features look and move almost, but not exactly, like natural human beings, it causes a response of revulsion among some human observers. The "valley" refers to the dip in a graph of the comfort level of humans as subjects move toward a healthy, natural human likeness described in a function of a subject's aesthetic acceptability. Examples can be found in the fields of robotics and 3D computer animation, among others."

~Wikipedia

This graph illustrates the uncanny valley:

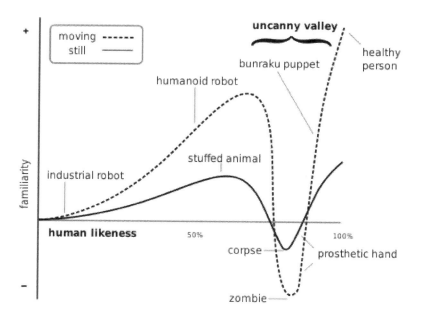

The psychopath I knew sometimes inhabited the area between bunraku puppet and zombie. But the majority of the time, he was pretty good at pulling it off. I was able to dismiss the Not-Quite-Sad faces and the Way-Too-Happy faces, but the Joker and the Corpse were traumatic and frightening. I knew when I saw them that they were absolutely genuine. At those times, his mask was off — and I was deep within the Uncanny Valley.

The uncanny valley effect not just limited to facial expressions — it also extends to the way someone moves, and also to the way they react to things. For example, if someone does not have a startle response when they hear a scream, it comes across as very disturbing.

Researchers say that in the uncanny valley, the human mind recognizes the subject as an obvious nonhuman, but then is attracted to it by the presence of human qualities. They're talking about robots and animations, but...

"The same reactive trajectory applies to narcissists and psychopaths: they are near-perfect imitations of humans, but lacking empathy and emotions. They are so close to being real, but they are just this shade of wrong."

~ "Peter Hale, Uncanny Valley, and Cold Empathy," Bizzaro Dopplepopolis

Since the uncanny valley is, at its core, a perception of lifelessness, *psychopaths probably perceive us as being in the uncanny valley, all the time.* Since they view us as no different from inanimate objects that they look upon with contempt, and see our behavior as bizarre, they may perceive all of us as uncanny. They may walk around seeing others as lifelike robots.

Do we worry about hurting a robot? No. They can't feel, after all. We have no empathy for robots because they're not human, because they're not alive. They exist to serve us, to fulfill our needs. If psychopaths can only see us as uncanny — as lifelike robots — it explains a lot.

It's ironic that we both see each other as being in the uncanny valley, isn't it?

"The uncanny valley, we think, is the perception of lifelessness, with the natural result being fear and disgust...This may be why, after being run down by a sociopath and realizing that the person has no moral wiring, we feel disgusted — the sociopath, to us, is in the uncanny valley. (Those of you who have experienced this know this kick-in-the-gut feeling)."

~ "Do Sociopaths See Everyone As Though In The Uncanny Valley?" Neurological Correlates

25 A HIDDEN FACT OF PSYCHOPATHS: THEY HAVE NO GENDER

Do psychopaths have a gender?

After my involvement with the psychopath, I got the strange feeling that he didn't really have a gender. When I learned that psychopaths have no identity — they only create one as needed — it started to make perfect sense. If they have no identity, it only seems logical that they don't have a gender identity either, doesn't it? It didn't seem to be an idea out of left field.

The psychopath in my life told me about many of his sexual exploits that happened 'a long time ago,' and he said that he'd had sex with men as well as women. I asked him if he was bisexual, and he said he was not. He said it was hard to explain. I had no idea at that time just how hard it would be to explain it.

This idea that he was genderless persisted, and it fascinated me. I felt sure psychopaths didn't identify with a gender, and I wanted some research to back it up. Surely, someone had to have studied this phenomena. In my quest, I plumbed the depths of the web for things like 'psychopaths and gender,' but I came up empty handed every time.

They definitely have a biological sex, according to their anatomy. But gender is psychological, and it refers to the sex a person self-identifies as. It's a social-sexual role.

But the one kind of person who will surely not identify in a fixed way with anything about themselves is the psychopath. So why would they identify with a gender?

I suspected that they present themselves to the world as masculine, feminine, heterosexual, homosexual, gay, lesbian, or transsexual, but underneath the façade they've chosen, they are genderless.

I set out once again to validate my suspicions, and this time, I found it. I only needed to look in a different place. Just as we talk and share information, so do psychopaths.

So, do psychopaths identify with a gender? Here is what some of them have to say about it:

"Personally, I am gender fluid and identify neutral."

"I don't see gender as being anything more than a biological difference. Much like the idea of morality, it is a social construct. What that means for me is the necessity to choose which side of the fence puts my talents to light to the best advantage..."

"Any research you found (on psychopaths and gender) would be skewed by the fact that the most oft interviewed psychopaths are criminals, and since society generally associates femininity with weakness, the intelligent male psychopath would naturally choose to portray a manly if not completely chauvinistic personality. The only honest psychopath is an anonymous psychopath..."

"Psychopaths of both genders tends to represent the gender they were born with because it is easier, and most people respond to that, rather than to the sexuality of minorities."

"I don't think that psychopaths struggle with their sexual identity at all. On the contrary, they seem to find it easy to play on both the feminine and the masculine sides in themselves."

"I'm trying to find something about it (gender and psychopaths) from research sources but there doesn't seem to be much to find so far. Maybe I've just been looking the wrong places, otherwise it would seem that we're on a wild goose chase."

"I haven't talked to anyone who falls under the psychopath spectrum that feels very feminine or masculine, when questioned. Most of the women seem very aggressive, and the males "sound" roughly the same, in how the present themselves...It just seems suspect to me that most of us don't feel very attached to one end or the other on the gender spectrum."

"Like others I've read about, I never took that diagnosis seriously... but so much has become clear to me, which before used to be a great mystery...one of those things is our tendency to not have an inherent sense of gender!"

"It's completely unimportant. Sexuality wise, I could go either way. I chose to portray myself in my real life as a homosexual for various reasons. I think what makes it impossible to delineate between how psychopaths view gender is our habit of being perpetually dishonest and chameleon-like. Were I a missionary I'd be the image of demure femininity, and were I in prison I would be as masculine as any testosterone-stuffed man."

"I have noticed that once we shed what has been called our 'Mask', the gender differences become less obvious."

"I've never felt attached to a gender role before. I consider my personality and attraction fairly androgynous."

26 ALL ABOUT FEMALE PSYCHOPATHS, FROM THE VICTIMS

Each time I rolled up my sleeves and set out to find out the facts about female psychopaths, I became frustrated. All I could find was a lot of conflicting information. Many experts say there are fewer female psychopaths than males...but some estimate there might actually be more. Some say they present differently. Others say the Psychopathy Checklist, considered a gold-standard test to measure psychopathy, is not accurate when used to evaluate females. There's even a theory that women diagnosed with other psychological disorders may actually be psychopathic:

"...new research suggests that some of the difference between men and women may not be in the existence of deceitful, manipulative, and exploitive personality traits but in the expression of them. Specifically, these researchers found that women may be more likely to express these personality deficits through behaviors that are typically associated with, and diagnosed as, other mental illnesses. For example, these researchers found overlap between some of the symptoms such as histrionic personality disorder or borderline personality disorder. A woman whose extreme fear of abandonment leads her to periodic outbursts of rage over real or imagined transgressions, flips between seeing her significant other as either completely perfect or totally evil, or who has to constantly be the center of attention certainly isn't who we think of when we think of the classic psychopath. But she may be just as incapable of true empathy, and just as manipulative and deceitful, as the callous, unemotional male."

~ Joni E. Johnston, Psy.D, "Female Psychopaths," Psychology Today.

Drs. Hare and Babiak discuss female psychopaths in their book, *Snakes In Suits:*

"Why aren't there any female psychopaths," an interviewer asked one of the authors. The fact that she could ask such a question reflects a curious wrinkle on sexism: the view, held by many people, that relatively few female psychopaths exists in society – or even prisons –and that those who do exist differ in fundamental ways from their male counterparts.

The issue is clouded by sex-role biases in the diagnosis of the disorder. Thus, when a female and a male each exhibit a psychopathic pattern of core personality traits – grandiose, egocentric, selfish, irresponsible, manipulative, deceitful, emotionally shallow, callous, and lacking in empathy, remorse, and guilt – a clinician will often diagnose the male as a psychopath (or antisocial personality disorder) and the female as something else, usually histrionic or narcissistic personality disorder.

In each case the clinician's diagnosis is influenced by expectations of how psychopaths should behave. That is, the clinician expects psychopaths to be tough, dominant, and aggressive, and a woman who does not project these characteristics therefore is not a psychopath. What the clinician fails to understand is that the behaviors of male and female psychopaths, like those of most other people, are shaped by the sex-role stereotypes cultivated by society. The same underlying personality structure may find different behavioral and social expression.

Although the process of socialization fails to embed in the network of inner controls we refer to collectively as conscience, it nevertheless makes them aware of society's expectations about sex-roles, of what is expected of them as men and women. More than most people, they effectively use these expectations as potent tools for manipulation. So a female psychopath might make full use of the passive, warm, nurturing, and dependent sex-role stereotype in order to get what she wants out of others..."

Men who have been involved with psychopathic females describe them best. From what they say, male and female psychopaths are remarkably similar and the damage they inflict is the same.

Here are their words. The following are all comments that were left on my website.

"I've just recently been attacked by a psychopath. We met many years ago and were great friends right off. We reconnected a little over a year ago some 25 years later. It was a long distance relationship where we saw each other every other weekend. This woman was my soul mate. Those words flowed often. We were so in tune with one another. Yes, the sex was over the top...magnificent! We would take out of town trips and go to concerts. She was spontaneous, free spirited, fun, sometimes ditzy, but she had a dark side -- she loves skeletons and psychological thrillers, mostly. She was into self help books, which now seems so odd as she was the picture-perfect presentation of love and caring. One of her favorite lines when writing or describing herself is "in loving kindness." *But her real game is heartbreak.* Like a serpent, she wound herself around every emotion and weakness I have. At the perfect moment, she cut me loose with no good reason. I hit the bottom hard and almost immediately afterwards, had a loaded pistol to my head. The pain was unbearable! Fortunately, I was able to apply some reasoning and delay my demise. About 2 weeks later after trying to sort through this, it dawned on me what I may be dealing with. Thanks to sites like this, I have no doubt that this woman is a full-blown Psychopath. The pain is gone as I now know what happened. The bad thing is, the next man might not be as insightful."

~

"I think my wife is a psychopath. I live in fear of going to jail, and of being heartbroken. She lies about me constantly. Since we've been married, every time we fight she becomes blind with rage. Very abusive verbally and physically. With as many excuses as you can think of to do so. I have a very strong feeling she is sexist as well. Whenever she doesn't "get her way" she calls my family, her relatives, the police, our neighbors…anyone that she can think of to create incredibly awkward and manipulative situations for me to look like I'm either doing something I'm not or being someone I'm not. I feel like I don't have any strength to leave her because I care about her. And because marriage is an important thing to me. But I'm just so desperately miserable. I mask it with music in my life… but I don't know how to live like this and be happy."

~

"My problem at this stage isn't understanding what happened so much as understanding why someone who I thought was lifelong companion would do it? And worst of all, where do I go from here? HOW do I go from here? I'm still reeling from this. I can't even believe it happened, let alone move on."

~

"I still can't believe it happened to me. My wife did so much harm I would bet most people who knew her on the surface wouldn't believe me. They would think I was jaded and mad because she discarded me, which I am. However, I would take a dozen polygraphs to state my case and clear up any misconceptions...

And this was -- and is -- a woman I love! How screwed up is that? I don't think she would spit on me if my hair were on fire! That's the hold she has. I know it's psychological and makes no sense. Yet that's the truth.

I miss the ideal I had in my head, not the many more times of emasculating, criticizing, lying, and gaslighting..."

~

"I now know that I was the victim of such a Psychopath. I am a man recently divorced and dealing with depression which has left me pretty vulnerable and open to abuse. I met this new woman on a night out and ended up back at her place that night on her insistence. She is a very confident, charming, intelligent and beautiful woman who had no problems socializing or reeling me in with her patter. The new "relationship" lasted just over two intense weeks where I found myself smothered with affection, adoration and intense sex. My "great qualities" were many and she was "falling" for me so easily that I missed the initial red flags, until one night something clicked in my head and nothing made sense. Everything about her became improbable and her stories sounded more and more exaggerated. Red flags were popping up everywhere and her intimate behavior and demeanor was starting to make me feel really unsettled, although I tried to ignore it. The Love Bombing, triangulation, the way she talked intimately about her past and other people so quickly, the questioning about my exes, her behavior out of context, etc. It was all there. I believe she saw a little of the turmoil in my head so she embarked on a new course of action to end the relationship, blaming her crazy ex for throwing a wrench in the works. At the end of a long and "deep" final conversation she acted so coldly and behaved so unconcerned in comparison to her words, and I knew I had been duped. Now I feel emotionally raped and unsettled. I am now questioning my own sanity and feel so upset that I have allowed this to happen to me just when I thought I was getting over my marriage breaking up. It sounds crazy that a two-week thing could be so intense and wrong, but it was. Women are just as capable of being psychopaths as are men..."

~

"I ran into a woman who is just for herself. She met me, used me, borrowed money, moved into my house, stole my money, and when I asked her to leave she moved out and went to police and charged me with mischief and assault. I am 58 years old and may end up in jail because I fell in love and felt sorry for her not having any place or anyone to help her."

~

"I've spent the weekend trying to reconnect with relatives (I had to go back three years in e-mail to find a phone number) and I found out that two months ago, when I was discarded, my ex called my sister-in-law to secretly tell her that she was leaving because I had been verbally abusive to her and she wanted to protect my daughter! She even prefaced it with saying that she should hear it from me instead of her, and to please not tell me that she told her and to wait for me to contact them. . .*really?* So my family has known for 2 months, been told I abused her, and hasn't reached out to me because she asked them not to?

... The pain of betrayal is unbearable. Even learning all I have I am completely bewildered....

My relative told me I should seek legal advice and begin documenting everything. I told her. I was scared to death to have her find out I was doing that. I feel completely defenseless against her. I feel powerless against her tactics and feel that anything I say or do is going to play into whatever her next sick plan is. I've been destroyed as a man and as a human being, and I don't think she's done yet."

~

"I feel completely alone, discarded, with all the strengths that made me who I was defeated. I keep reminding myself of a saying I once heard, that bravery is not acting without fear -- bravery is acting when you are afraid.

… Sometimes I feel like I can't breathe, like the walls are closing in…I found the courage to tell her I didn't feel I was being treated fairly (emotionally, love, compassion, consideration, etc.) and she needed to decide if she really wanted to be with me. Of course, I suffered the usual wrath that I knew would follow, about how invalid my thoughts and feelings were and how it was all my fault… She had proven over the years she had no capacity for empathy (even once saying her brain was wired differently from mine). Even knowing she would never feel any compassion for where she's left me, I can't stop thinking how could she do this? Doesn't she know what she's doing to me, to us, to our daughter? I know the answer, and now I'm beginning to understand why, but it doesn't help at all with this searing pain of loss and of being discarded.

It's embarrassing to even speak about, and I know I'll be put under a microscope to even suggest that I might have been abused, since I am the man in the relationship. I had mentioned to her several times over the years I felt I was being emotionally abused and she would roll on the floor laughing hysterically at me, saying something to the effect that I was a wimp to even say it, since I was the man, and a woman can't abuse a man.

Nearly every article I've read on this has described my relationship with her exactly, right to the part where I feel like no one is going to believe me. I left the dream job I had worked toward for twenty years, one year after meeting her. I've bought three houses up and down the east coast, had five different jobs, and my finances are destroyed. All, I thought, because I loved her so much it was my job to do what would make her happy. Now, six years from being eligible for retirement, I will begin paying child support and won't be the normal "Daddy" I thought I was going to be. A decision made for me.

…She told me the first week we began our "love" affair that she wanted me to father her children, that she wanted a daughter. She wanted to take care of me when I got old, told me I would never be alone again, and said she would never leave me. At least I know now this was the "love-bombing" phase. I kept hoping that once-in-a-lifetime love I had would return one day, it never did. Literally overnight, when the love-bombing ended, I asked what was going on and her response was 'the relationship has progressed.'

When she was married to her first husband she initiated contact with me (I was the friend of a friend), confided how she had been abused, and said she really connected with me. I was her soul-mate, her savior. I swore I never would be involved with a married woman, but she made me believe we were meant to be together. She said so many things that left me in shock, like I was a character in a movie where my deepest fantasies of finding my true love were unfolding. I was absolutely convinced. I'm a warm, loving, nurturing person by nature. I was physically and emotionally strong before we met. I was in touch with my feelings and confident in my capacity to respect the feelings of others. I'm now an emotional train wreck, with numerous stress related illness and completely isolated from my old social support network. I feel ashamed that I couldn't stop it, and my self-esteem is long gone.

I'm certain she is telling her friends and family that she is getting out of an abusive relationship, the same thing she told everyone when she sought me out while she was still married to and living with her first husband. She was physically abusive in the beginning and rationalized it as the result of her abusive relationship with her husband. The physical things stopped (grabbing me by the ear and yelling into the side of my head, etc.), but the tirades never did. I thought I was the strong man, there to let her vent and heal, and that she needed compassion for the hell she had been through, which I doubt now was even close to the stories she told. I'm embarrassed to speak of this to anyone and I don't know where to go.

I have a hard time ever asking for help, and now I feel like I have to justify myself to even ask.

The number of incidents of cold, callous behavior would fill a novel. I just really needed to tell it to someone…"

~

"My life has been completely ruined several times. At 54, I am having to have faith that somehow I can start again after psychopaths have stolen everything from me that I worked so hard to create: an emotional healthy attitude and financial wealth…If I gave the details, anyone with any knowledge would know I have lived a living hell. I find it hard to trust anyone anymore, or function, though I must and I am worried because I am tired and breaking down physically. I have to pray that I don't become homeless and starving because with the zeitgeist of our time, it's likely."

~

"I started dating a sociopath a little more than two years ago, the summer when I was 18 and she was 17. We met through a mutual friend, and she rushed the relationship while I wanted to take it slow. For the longest time I considered that one of the best summers of my life because of how euphoric she made it all out to be. I stopped hanging out with pretty much all of my friends and started neglecting my family, all the while just spending more and more time with her.

Then I started college at a university about an hour and a half away from where I live, and she started her senior year of high school. What I didn't know was she had already reeled me in. Things were fine at first, we thought we could make it work for a year until she graduated. But everything changed about midway through the semester. She became distant, and never wanted to talk anymore. But I had been home to see her every damn weekend and most Wednesdays we met in between to eat and do other things. She blamed me for our relationship being so awful. She said it was my fault we were so far apart because I went to a school an hour and a half away, when there was a community college I could be going to about 30 minutes from where she lived. I tried to explain to her I made the decision to go there months before I even met her. She didn't care.

I would finally make it home for the weekend and then things would be fine. Until Sunday night. When it was time for me to leave she would cry and pitch fits, not letting me leave until 1 AM or later, with an hour and a half drive to my dorm and an 8 AM class. She didn't care. It was all about her.

Then her crying and sobbing on Sunday nights got worse. She began to start fights and try to leave me over stupid things, but because she knew how much I cared for her she knew I wouldn't leave until I "fixed things", which involved sitting there telling her how amazing she was and how ugly, stupid, and annoying any girl I had ever been with in my past was.

During the week, all I did was lay in my dorm and wait for her to call. I pretty much had two friends my whole freshman year of college: my roommate, and a cousin who lived in the area. This was strange for me because in high school I was a very sociable person. (I played varsity football, basketball, and baseball, and received an academic scholarship to the university I attend). She completely changed who I was. I hated myself but I loved her. I had no idea there were people like her in the world.

My dad finally intervened the summer after my freshman year. He told me he would kick me out and never help me out financially again unless I ended it with her. I knew he was right, but I just couldn't explain the hurt I felt when I tried to leave her. He and the rest of my friends and family just could NOT understand. I finally left her. I went into a rampant alcoholic stage, at the age of 19. Things started to get better and I started getting off the bottle until (at this point it had been about four months since I had talked to or seen her) we got back in contact. What a stupid and life changing mistake that was!

We dated in secret until February of this year, until I found a strong core of new friends who helped me end it. She had actually taken an attempt at my life, which just totally blew my mind. I realized she was mentally sick and un-healable. I told my dad of our secrecy and he was pretty pissed, but he understood. I was finally done with her for good.

Until she came to me a month later with a signed piece of paper from a doctor saying she was 2 months pregnant. I said, "I thought you said you were on the pill!! What the hell?! How did this happen?"

"I lied," she said.

Such a simple yet life changing statement.

My daughter is almost a month old now. I am still not with her, and she is engaged to some other poor soul now. We are about to start an extreme custody battle. I feel like I've been through the hell of a lifetime, but the hell has only just began. It's just so much to handle, yet I do my best to stay positive. How can I deal with all this? And

116

by the way, I'm 20 now and still in college. So I'm cursed to make that Godforsaken drive every other weekend to see my little girl, and I'll have to see the sociopath who changed my life…"

~

"There are an equal amount of female psychopaths out there as male ones. Females tend to fly under society's radar as they are less likely to commit criminal offences, just moral ones. I have two children with a female psychopath who has used as tools to dismantle my life and my soul, and she greatly enjoyed herself in the process. This enjoyment of cruelty is the hard fact to come to terms with, and it baffles us all.

They are very good at creating a good impression of themselves and portraying their victim as the real culprit. This is what really gets me. I've been in hell and everybody thinks I'm the onster……….except a few who have had experience themselves."

~

"I never knew such a thing as emotional rape existed until my relationship with a sociopath ended. We were only together for two years but the constant onslaught of lies, deceit, emotional swings, lack of reciprocity, and personality shifts turned things sour in a real hurry. I was always at fault because I would react to being lied to or saw a lack of reciprocity. I've had the police called on me for no reason twice, almost had my vehicle stolen and house seized. You don't realize what's happening in this scenario because you love this person so much and will take any and all abuse to try and maintain the relationship. We've been apart for a month and I'm just starting to see and feel the ill effects of this toxic relationship. I have trouble sleeping, night sweats, severe anxiety, and an overt lack of a sense of self. I was used in every imaginable way, and now I feel like I've been robbed of my person, my soul, my mind, and my being. To make matters worse, she has her masters in psychology…

…May God have mercy on that woman's soul."

27 The Nemesis of the Psychopath: BOREDOM

The thought of a bored psychopath is kind of scary. And yet the thought of a psychopath who isn't bored is kind of scary, too. Seriously, though, psychopaths have a real problem with boredom. They become bored very easily, and they can't tolerate it.

Boredom is an ongoing 'mood' in a psychopath's life, one they are constantly trying to relieve. And relieve it they will, in one way or another.

Why do psychopaths become bored so easily?

They require intense stimulation in order to feel anything, to become excited, or to have fun. Because of this, nothing is really satisfying and nothing can keep their interest for very long. Their restless, relentless search for the stimulation they need is an ongoing pursuit. It hounds them continually, like the meaningless and destructive drive of an addiction.

For us, boredom is usually experienced as a passing mood of impatience and dissatisfaction, along with a vague want of something unknown. We find thoughts or activities that fill the moment.

In contrast, the conscious experience of boredom in the psychopath is a complex emotional state, one of the few they can feel. It is both chronic and acute. Psychopathic boredom is described as a continual restless and dysphoric feeling, acted out through aggressive and hypomanic activity. They experience boredom as a sense of restlessness and emptiness that is ever-present.

Boredom is felt intensely during idle moments when psychopaths have exhausted their 'supply' and are left by themselves after their existing sources (victims) have been devalued. During these times, the psychopath goes on an aggressive pursuit for more. Since they have no conscience, they are uninhibited in their search for relief.

When a psychopath is bored, he may recognize that his grandiosity is only an illusion. This recognition is unbearable, according to Reid Meloy, PhD., and he experiences a need for immediate and aggressive gratification to restore his grandiosity.

Psychopaths experience chronic boredom because they empty the world of meaningful relationships through devaluation.

'Need for Stimulation/Proneness to Boredom' is an item on the Psychopathy Checklist, a diagnostic scale that measures the presence and severity of psychopathy.

How do psychopaths themselves describe their experience of boredom?

Here is one psychopath's description:

"So what's my problem? As I fiddle with the Sharpie in my mouth, twisting and scraping it against my canines, I ponder my own question. What is my problem? I can't imagine what could be bothering me. Maybe it's just the weather.

Some people sob at the softest mention of cancer within. All I can say is there is a much more sinister disease burbling in this demonic blood of mine: Boredom. And it afflicts me. Rotting my eyeballs inside, then out. Setting my skin on fire and then dousing it with ice...

Boredom is the Devil and I am fucking possessed."

And another's:

"The words 'uninspired' and 'restless' describe very well what I call boredom.

To them it looks like I am easily bored, but to me it looks very different. They think I get bored because I have a shallow emotional life and need stronger impact from sensations because of this.

But what they call 'bored,' I call a greater need for inspiration."

As victims, we were just temporary relief from the psychopath's crushing boredom. We provided a bit of the 'inspiration' needed to relieve their endless ennui, and we restored their sense of grandiosity.

Nothing more than that.

28 THE STRANGER ACROSS THE KITCHEN TABLE

One day the psychopath I was involved with smiled broadly and said,

"We get along great for two strangers, don't we?"

My immediate reaction was one of being completely stunned, which turned quickly into hurt and bewilderment. Strangers? We weren't strangers, far from it! We were soul mates, after all. I felt as if I'd been punched in the gut.

When all was said and done and I realized he was psychopathic, I thought for sure he made that statement purposely to hurt me. And maybe he did, but one thing is clear now — *it was the truth*. No one is more than a stranger to a psychopath. Without the ability to bond with others, they remain permanently and significantly disconnected. They are true loners.

Psychopaths are also strangers to us. We can never know who they really are until we see beneath their carefully constructed mask, and when we finally do, we realize they are not at all who they seemed to be.

You may have heard of James Fallon, a neuroscientist and author of the book *The Psychopath Inside: A Neuroscientist's Personal Journey into the Dark Side of the Brain*. In the course of his research, Fallon discovered that he himself had a psychopathic brain and that he had many traits of psychopathy (although he does not consider himself a 'full-blown' psychopath).

In an interview published in the Atlantic, "Life as a Nonviolent Psychopath," Fallon describes his relationship with those closest to him. When explaining how he interacts with his wife, sister and mother, he said "Even though they've always been close to me, I don't treat them all that well. *I treat strangers pretty well* — really well, and people tend to like me when they meet me — *but I treat my family the same way, like they're just somebody at a bar.* I treat them well, but I don't treat them in a special way. That's the big problem....They absolutely expect and demand more. It's a kind of cruelty, a kind of abuse, because you're not giving them that love."

When the psychopath I knew enthusiastically exclaimed that we sure got along great for two strangers, he may have really been pleased as punch -- since that's the most he was capable of, and the most he could ever give, or get, from a relationship.

But as non-psychopaths, we need close relationships with people truly capable of loving and connecting. To believe we are loved by someone — and then to find out we are no more than a stranger to them — is deeply shocking and disturbing.

None of us wants to believe the person we loved was actually a stranger to us, just as we were to them. But understanding how the psychopathic mind works can help you move forward after the relationship comes to an end; when you realize you were dealing with someone who was so fundamentally different, it can help resolve lingering feelings of confusion.

29 FEAR AND MANIPULATION: PERFECT TOGETHER

Fear is the best way to set someone up for manipulation.

That's exactly what happened to us when we were involved in a 'relationship' with a psychopath. In the process of the psychopathic bond, the moment when the joy at finding love turns into the fear of losing it is called the 'manipulative shift.' When that happens, the mayhem begins.

We think love is what makes us vulnerable, but it's actually the fear of losing that love that puts us most at risk.

In order to manipulate us, the psychopath had to cause fear. In order to cause fear, he had to first create the illusion of love. But fear was the key to our downfall.

Fear is a primal human state. It begins in childhood, even if no real danger exists. We fear monsters hiding in the closet or under the bed.

Fear robs us of our ability to think rationally. Psychopaths (who do not experience fear) know this, and they use it to great effect — not only in relationships, but in societies.

What got me thinking about fear was the debacle of hysteria surrounding the Ebola virus disease — in particular, the events surrounding nurse Kaci Hickox's return from the hot zone — and the very scary places that fear was leading us. It was not Ebola we should have feared — it is fear we should fear, because it makes us easy to manipulate. When we're afraid, whether that fear is real or imagined, we want to return to safety. When we believe someone can do that, we sigh with relief instead of thinking critically about what's really going on.

Irrational fear was building in the US as misinformation and gaps in knowledge caused panic. Many people believed that infected but asymptomatic people could spread Ebola to the public by riding planes, buses, and subways, going bowling, or going out to dinner, even though there was no factual basis for that.

In response to that irrational fear, the governors of NJ and NY saw an opportunity for personal gain instead of an opportunity for education. They started talking about mandatory quarantines for health workers returning from West Africa. The advice of health experts was disregarded as they announced they would be the ones who would protect us. Even though public health experts said there was no risk to the public, we were told it was 'better to be safe than sorry.'

Just as Kaci Hickox arrived at an airport in NJ, the governor put his ill-conceived plan into action. Kaci was stopped at customs and held for several hours. Then, she was transported by an ambulance escorted by eight police cars with lights flashing and sirens blaring (unbelievable but true) to a hospital where she was supposed to be detained for 21 days. But she wasn't even taken *into* the hospital — no, it had to be more dramatic than that to build up the fear factor. She was put in a tent — *a tent!* — without running water, which meant no shower or flushing toilet. Her belongings were taken and she was given paper clothing. For two days, she was denied access to an attorney.

When Kaci spoke out in complaint, the comments about her were shocking: Kaci was a prima dona and a selfish bitch who should just shut up and deal with it. Some hoped she would die.

Last I heard, even murderers get flushing toilets, cloth garments and access to an attorney. But this health professional — who received a joint master's degree from the Johns Hopkins schools of Public Health and Nursing — wasn't deemed worthy of those things. We know that if we stop the spread of Ebola in Africa it also stops the spread to other places, which makes it a matter of national security. No different from a soldier, Kaci went to the front lines of a horrific battle and put her own life on the line to stop the threat.

But what she returned to was hardly the hero's welcome she deserved.

I've been an RN for years, and I've also learned some things about manipulation, so I saw the truth of what was happening in gory detail. I found it both fascinating and terrifying. I was fairly sure her detention wouldn't stand, since coercive measures like mandatory quarantine of people exhibiting no symptoms of an illness, and when not medically necessary, is illegal and raises serious constitutional concerns about the state abusing its powers. But you never know. When people are afraid, strange things can happen.

The overwhelming support for her illegal detainment was staggering.

The general public seemed to think it was a great idea. The governor was keeping them safe from 'selfish and dangerous' public health professionals like Hickox, whom he said 'could not be trusted' to self-monitor and take action at the first sign of symptoms. After all, everyone could see just how selfish they were, as evidenced by their selfless service to desperately ill people in a situation most of us would consider hell on earth... If the governor says so, then it must be true.

When we're afraid, a manipulator can talk us out of the truth we see right in front of us. Words become more real than reality.

The governor said he was "sorry she was ill" and hoped she'd recover soon, even though she was not ill. He even said she was "obviously ill," when she wasn't ill at all. He said he was "sorry for the inconvenience," but he had to keep the public safe. He knew the power of a few well-chosen words and phrases that would stick in the public's mind.

The governor who forcibly detained a citizen without cause said he "had no remorse" and he would do it again. When someone tells you something about themselves, believe it the first time.

What this self-serving 'public servant' was really doing was using the public's fear to gain political power.

He wasn't really keeping anyone safe, and he knew it. He was manipulating them for personal gain, with his eye on the 2016 presidential election.

For personal gain, he exploited the public's fear. He not only exploited it — he actually made it worse. For personal gain, he stripped a citizen of her freedom and civil rights by forcibly detaining her for no justifiable reason and denying her access to an attorney. For personal gain, he undermined the public's trust in healthcare professionals by saying they could not be trusted to monitor themselves, and he undermined the public's trust in public health officials and in science when he told us we couldn't believe what they told us about the virus. In doing so, the governor implied that he was the only one who was worthy of our trust, and he was the only one who could keep us safe.

Never underestimate the power of fear to prime us for manipulation.

When Kaci was freed from her illegal detention she went home to Maine, where she was supposed to comply with a voluntary quarantine by isolating herself in her home. She refused. She knew she wouldn't pose a threat to the public. A judge then ruled she could not be forcibly quarantined because there was no legally or medically justifiable reason to do so.

I started to compare this whole fiasco to the personal experience of being victimized by a psychopath, and I realized this:

Fear takes away our ability to think clearly. It causes us to give our power away to someone else if we believe they can remove the threat. When we see someone as being 'the one' who is able to take our fear away, we will give them just about anything. And we won't even realize it while it's happening.

When we were fearful of losing our relationship with the psychopath, by default he became the only one who could remove that fear. That made us hand him all of our power and give him complete control.

I've come to the conclusion we should consider fear a major red flag that we might be involved with a psychopath. The next time we're in a relationship and we feel fearful of losing it, we need to let that alert us to the fact that something is seriously wrong. We also need to remember that we can't think clearly when we feel fear. We need to pause and look at our fear by carefully observing reality.

If we don't do these things we will give up our freedom and our power, and we will come to regret it.

THE ONLY THING WE HAVE TO FEAR

IS FEAR ITSELF

30 IDENTIFYING A PSYCHOPATH: TWENTY SUBTLE AND HIDDEN SIGNS

Invisibility is the most disturbing thing about psychopathy.

Psychopaths must keep their true nature hidden, and they know how to do it. They're skilled actors and mimics. After all, they can only dupe us if they can first make us believe they're honest, genuine, and trustworthy. To do that, they have to come across as "normal." When they slip up, they're good at explaining it away, distracting us, or shifting the blame. But they also give clues to their real identify.

Caution is advised, though, because psychopaths may not give us the clues we expect or we may miss those clues. While our experience and knowledge are sure to protect us to some extent, over-confidence is never a good idea. Even Dr. Robert Hare, psychopathy expert extraordinaire, admits that with all his experience he could still be duped by a predatory psychopath. "In short interactions," he says, "anyone can be duped."

Twenty Subtle Or Hidden Signs That You Might Be Dealing With A Psychopath

1. **They have a demeanor of black-leather toughness combined with boyish innocence,** according to psychologist Kevin Dutton. You may have a feeling that he or she is street-smart, tough-minded, or has been around the block more than once, while at the same time you sense a girlish or boyish innocence. This is one of the first things I noticed about the psychopath I knew, before I even spoke to him.

2. **They embody incongruity.** This is a big one. The example above is just one possible manifestation of an *overall pattern* of incongruity or contradiction the psychopath usually displays. He or she may contradict themselves from one sentence to the next...or it may take a few weeks or months for a completely different point of view to emerge. He may express seemingly deep sympathy for the plight of the homeless, and then question contemptuously how anyone could become so 'worthless,' like mine did. This pattern of incongruity runs throughout all aspects of their behavior. A classic example is the hot-cold, sweet-mean way they act with us. Watch for incongruity, and run far and fast if you see it.

3. **They exude a subtle but definite air of confidence and superiority.** Their body language reads as 'haughty.' Their physical posture gives off vibes of "superiority, hidden powers and amused indifference," says psychopath Sam Vaknin.

4. They tell you stories of shady or unsavoury things they do or did 'in the past.' Psychopaths love to tell the tales of their business or sexual exploits, but you may feel convinced they're not 'that way' any longer.

5. **They need little sleep.** Psychopaths are always on the go in their quest for stimulation. They're busy, busy, busy. They may sleep just four or five hours per night.

6. **They sometimes exhibit unconvincing emotional responses.** Most of the time they may come across as genuine, but at other times you may get the feeling that they're a bit 'off' or even engaging in poor play-acting.

7. **They can go from being extremely angry to totally calm in a matter of minutes.** Emotions are shallow and short-lived for a psychopath.

8. **They will drop hints of their true nature, but in a veiled manner.** These hints are also called 'tells.' For example, if a psychopath is taking advantage of your trusting nature, he may say "You would be so easy for a con artist to dupe, because you're way too trusting." Why do they do this? When psychopaths put one over on someone, they experience *duping delight*, which is pleasure at having someone within their control and being able to manipulate them. Or they may do it to add a little more excitement to their 'game,' because it increases the odds that they could get caught. When they do this, it means they're bored and ready to move on.

8. **They may be hairy from the neck down, with some degree of baldness up top.** This is due to a high testosterone level. Females may show signs of being alarmingly aggressive underneath their feminine demeanor. Both sexes have a high sex drive.

10. **They have deviant sexual desires, and they want you to fulfill them.** Plenty of normal people have these desires, too, but a psychopath will be more aggressive in fulfilling them.

"Individuals with deviant sexual preferences and normal levels of empathy, kindness, and self-control have many strategies for satisfying their needs, including negotiation, compromise, and restraint; however, individuals with high levels of psychopathic traits might turn to sexually aggressive strategies to attain gratification." From the article, 'In Psychopaths, The Line Between Fantasy And Reality Is Thin'

11. **They have a poor sense of smell.** "Individuals who scored highly on psychopathic traits were more likely to struggle to both identify smells and tell the difference between smells, even though they knew they were smelling something," according to findings by researchers Mehmet Mahmut and Richard Stevenson of Macquarie University in Australia.

12. **Their speech is filled with disfluencies.** Psychopaths may use phrases like "uh" or "umm" a lot to break up their speech. The exact reason for this isn't clear, but researchers speculate that they might be trying harder to make a positive impression, needing more mental effort and time to frame (or make up) a story.

13. **They can't describe an emotion or their personal experience of one.** Psychopaths fail to understand the fundamental nature of emotions, such as fear or love. Psychopaths can mimic an emotion or tell you they're experiencing it, but if you dig deeper and ask them to describe how they feel, they'll become lost or even frustrated. They're like a blind person trying to understand what others mean when they talk about color. One reader told me that after her psychopathic boyfriend told her he loved her, she asked him what love meant to him. After giving it some thought, he said "If you and I were stranded alone together on another planet, I probably wouldn't want to kill you."

In his book *Without Conscience, Dr. Robert Hare* describes an interview with a psychopathic offender who can't seem to understand the fundamental nature of fear:

"When I rob a bank," he said, "I notice that the teller shakes or becomes tongue-tied. One barfed all over the money. She must have been pretty messed up inside, but I don't know why. If someone pointed a gun at me, I guess I'd be afraid but I wouldn't throw up." When asked to describe how he would feel in such a situation, his reply contained no references to bodily sensations. He said things such as, "I'd give you the money"; "I'd think of ways to get the drop on you"; "I'd try and get my ass out of there." When asked again how he would *feel,* not what he would think or do, he seemed perplexed. Asked if he ever felt his heart pound or his stomach churn, he replied, "Of course! I'm not a robot. I really get pumped up when I have sex or when I get into a fight."

14. **They have a diminished startle response.** This is apparently related to decreased activity in the amygdala, a structure in the brain related to fear and other emotions. If you're walking down the street with a beau and he or she doesn't flinch when a car backfires, watch out.

15. **They participate in dangerous or extreme sports and activities.** Psychopaths may get their thrills from flying lessons, BASE jumping, brain surgery (hopefully only if they're a qualified neurosurgeon!), driving fast, juggling machetes, or carelessly cheating on their wives. In order to feel excitement, psychopaths need high risk and intensity.

16. **They invade your personal space.** We all have a certain distance we keep between ourselves or others, which is usually culturally determined. But the psychopath may stand extra close, within your personal space. Surprisingly, researchers found that *coldheartedness* was the a significant predictor of preferred distance, with higher scores associated with preference for *shorter* distances.

The study's authors wrote, "Consistent with our hypothesis, results showed that coldheartedness scores (which index interpersonal callousness) significantly predicted preferred distance, with more callous participants showing a preference for shorter distances. We speculate that interpersonal distance preferences of highly callous individuals may mediate the *relationship between callous traits and aggression,* by producing behaviors that facilitate aggressive behavior." This pattern is probably linked to abnormal amygdala functioning. From the article, 'Don't Stand So Close To Me: Psychopathy and The Regulation of Interpersonal Distance'

17. **They have an eerily calm demeanor.**

18. **They have a saintly aura.** Of course, it's one they create for themselves. They may engage in phony altruism by donating to or volunteering for a cause, or hand out dollars to needy people on the street. If you weren't there to witness it, they'll be sure to tell you all about it later while smiling beatifically and waiting for your admiration.

19. **They speak prolifically and even poetically.** As master wordsmiths, they can deliver running monologues that are frequently intriguing. Or they may deliver a soliloquy like an actor alone on a stage, while ignoring your attempts to respond.

20. **They have little to no body odor.** This is purely anecdotal, but I've heard many victims report this. Your mileage may vary.

31 THE MISSING PIECE OF THE PUZZLE

As I read all I could find about psychopathy, I found something was missing.

A key piece of the puzzle was consistently absent, and it bothered me. I wasn't sure how much this missing piece even mattered, but it seemed important enough to make me search for it and ponder it, and to come up with a possibility of my own.

We are told that psychopathic people don't have a conscience, that they can't feel love or remorse, and that they don't experience empathy as we do. I understand that, but it raises some questions.

Is our conscience and our ability to experience love, remorse and empathy the only things that keep us from hurting others? As far as I know, I don't even have any desire to hurt anyone. If I *did* have such desires I could understand how these qualities would stop me from acting on them, but I don't have them and I don't think the majority of people do, either.

So, then, does the lack of these qualities (conscience, love, remorse, empathy) in the psychopath somehow *cause* dark impulses to arise? That doesn't seem to make sense.

Or are the two unrelated, such as that a psychopath lacks these qualities *and* has abnormal impulses to hurt others? I've never read anywhere that psychopathy causes the brain to generate thoughts of harm; I've only read that psychopaths lack those qualities, probably due to psychopathy being a neurological disorder in which the emotional parts of the brain are not connected to the executive, or thinking, parts.

But I haven't read anywhere that this disengagement within the brain causes thoughts of harm to arise, or is related to it in any way. In fact, so far I've never seen the issue of 'the origin of thoughts of harm' addressed in anything I've read or heard about psychopathy. Did I miss it? And does it really matter? Would it make a difference? Maybe not, but I'm curious about it anyway.

The origin of these "thoughts of harm" are the missing piece of the puzzle for me.

If the thoughts and desires to harm others weren't there, a psychopathic person would not be any more dangerous than anyone else. They would still be unable to experience love or empathy or remorse and still be unable to bond with others, so they wouldn't be the best choice for a close friend or partner or parent. But they wouldn't be dangerous.

There is a theory that the behavior of psychopathic people depends on the environment they were raised in. If they're raised by abusive parents, for example, they can turn out to be abusive themselves (neurotypical people are also at risk of the same fate). But if they are raised in a loving and supportive environment, they may turn out to be what's known as a 'pro-social' psychopath, or a psychopath who does not purposely harm others. This theory may explain it. Maybe...

But I can't help thinking maybe there's something more to it.

What about the ones who *do* grow up in loving and supportive homes, but grow to be anti-social psychopaths anyway? I've read about children who are described as 'callous-unemotional' (a psychopathy diagnosis is not given to children, but this term means basically the same thing). These kids do things like torture family pets, seriously injure siblings, and cause all kinds of chaos within a family. There's a fascinating article on the subject titled 'Can You Call a 9-Year-Old a Psychopath?'

Here's an excerpt:

"By the time he turned five, Michael had developed an uncanny ability to switch from full-blown anger to moments of pure rationality or calculated charm — a facility that Anne describes as deeply unsettling. 'You never know when you're going to see a proper emotion,' she said.....Over the last six years, Michael's parents have taken him to eight different therapists and received a proliferating number of diagnoses......Then last spring, the psychologist treating Michael referred his parents to Dan Waschbusch, a researcher at Florida International University. Following a battery of evaluations, Anne and Miguel were presented with another possible diagnosis: their son Michael might be a psychopath...'This isn't like autism, where the child and parents will find support....Even if accurate, it's a ruinous diagnosis. No one is sympathetic to the mother of a psychopath.

....Another psychologist described one boy who used a knife to cut off the tail of the family cat bit by bit, over a period of weeks. The boy was proud of the serial amputations, which his parents initially failed to notice...In another famous case, a 9-year-old boy...pushed a toddler into the deep end of a motel swimming pool in Florida. As the boy struggled and sank to the bottom, the boy pulled up a chair to watch. Questioned by the police afterward, he explained that he was curious to see someone drown......Mark Dadds, a psychologist at the University of New South Wales who studies antisocial behavior in children, acknowledges that 'no one is comfortable labeling a five-year-old a psychopath.' But, he says, ignoring these traits may be worse. 'The research showing that this temperament exists and can be identified in young children is quite strong.'"

This article, like the others, still does not address the missing piece of the puzzle — where do thoughts of cutting off a cat's tail, or watching someone drown, come from? Why is there an urge to do harm when empathy and remorse are missing? Where does it come from, and why is it there?

What I wonder is this: Could it be that we all have these dark thoughts emanating from somewhere deep within our brains, but they are kept from our conscious awareness by our conscience, which acts as a gatekeeper? Is it possible that our conscience acts as a defense mechanism to protect ourselves from acknowledging we have these thoughts, in order to keep our self-image intact? After all, these thoughts would be unacceptable to us and would be disturbing enough to disrupt our ability to function and to live our day-to-day lives and maintain close relationships.

And in the psychopath, since that gatekeeper — the conscience — is not present, does it then mean that those dark thoughts are let into their conscious awareness and are thus available for their consideration, unstopped by empathy or love if they decide to act on them?

32 Is There a "Psycho" In a Psychopath?

"It turns out that an eerie type of chaos can lurk just behind a facade of order – and yet, deep inside the chaos lurks an even eerier type of order"

~ Douglas Hostadter

Are psychopaths psychotic?

It is said that psychopaths aren't insane, because they have an absence of delusions and other signs of irrational thinking. Is this correct? Something about it doesn't seem quite right.

"The term 'psychosis' is very broad and can mean anything from relatively normal aberrant experiences through to the complex and catatonic expressions of schizophrenia and bipolar type 1 disorder. In properly diagnosed psychiatric disorders...psychosis is a descriptive term for the hallucinations, delusions, sometimes violence, and impaired insight that may occur. Psychosis is generally given to noticeable deficits in normal behavior and more commonly to diverse types of hallucinations or delusional beliefs, especially as regards the relation between self and others as in grandiosity and paranoia." ~ Wikipedia

Hmmm...do psychopaths have delusions? Check. Are they sometimes violent? Check. Is their insight impaired? Check. Are they grandiose? Check. Do they have deficits in normal behavior (they might not be 'noticeable,' but they're definitely there)? Check.

Couldn't a psychopath's pathological sense of grandiosity be considered a *delusion* of grandeur?

"A delusion of grandeur is the fixed, false belief that one possesses superior qualities such as genius, fame, omnipotence, or wealth. It is most often a symptom of schizophrenia, but can also be a symptom found in psychotic or bipolar disorders, as well as dementia (such as Alzheimer's)." John M. Grohol, Psy.D.

Consider that psychopaths believe humans are objects. Because of that belief, they feel free to manipulate, use, and discard with impunity. Isn't that delusional?

Ted Bundy, the psychopathic serial killer, said "Sometimes I feel like a vampire." The psychopath I was involved with also told me he was a vampire. That seems delusional to me.

Speaking of Ted Bundy — who viciously murdered up to 100 people — I have to wonder how he could *not* be insane. Does a sane person kill others for sport because they have absolutely no regard for their humanity? Not that I know of. Because Bundy was an 'organized' serial killer — his crimes were not spur-of-the-moment-decisions, they were carefully planned and executed — he didn't fit the definition of psychotic. But even so, can that be considered 'rational thinking?' He was intelligent and articulate, had a degree in psychology, and was handsome and clean cut. His persona gave no clue to his 'deficits in normal behavior,' but that doesn't mean those deficits weren't there.

Because outward signs of their disorder are missing, psychopathy is virtually ignored by the mental health profession.

"Psychopaths don't exhibit the manias, hysterias, and neuroses that are present in other types of mental illness. Their main defect, what psychologists call 'severe emotional detachment — a total lack of empathy and remorse — is concealed, and harder to describe than the symptoms of schizophrenia or bipolar disorder. This absence of easily readable signs has led to debate among mental-health practitioners about what qualifies as psychopathy and how to diagnose it. Psychopathy isn't identified as a disorder in the *Diagnostic and Statistical Manual of Mental Disorders*, the American Psychiatric Association's canon; instead, a more general term, antisocial personality disorder covers the condition."

From the New Yorker article "Suffering Souls," about the work of psychopathy researcher Dr. Kent Kiehl.

Kiehl says he is "frustrated by the lack of respect shown to psychopathy by the mental-health establishment." Because of it, he says, hardly anyone is funding research into the science.

Dr. Robert Hare also disagrees with psychopathy being classified as antisocial personality disorder. He says, "It's like having pneumonia versus having a cold. They share some common symptoms, but one is much more virulent." Hare sees his work as warning society of a devastating and costly mental disorder that it mostly continues to ignore.

In his first edition of *The Mask of Sanity*, Hervey M. Cleckley described his psychopathic patients as "frankly and unquestionably psychotic," but modified this in later editions. He came to agree with other professionals who felt it would stretch the definition of psychosis too far. "However at various other points he still suggested that, despite 'traditional' classification, *the extent of the inner abnormality and associated dysfunction in psychopathy is such that it might be considered as psychosis in many respects.*" Wikipedia

One psychopath described his mental state not as insanity, but as '*forming models of reasoning that are different from the norm.*' He attributed this to a lack of emotional attachment to common ideas and accepted values. Might that mean a lack of attachment to reality?

What confuses the issue is that psychopaths do know right from wrong, but they don't care. That may be true, but it muddies things up and makes it seem that they can act differently if only they would choose to. But then we turn around and agree they have a serious mental disorder called psychopathy that is responsible for their lack of a conscience, their inability to feel remorse, and their inability to love or care about others. Which is it — are they just like normal people who make bad choices and who could change if they wanted to, or do they have a mental or neurological disorder? How can it be both?

Maybe psychopathy is a psychosis, one that the afflicted person is able to conceal. That doesn't make sense, but it seems to describe it. In the 1940s, there was a psychiatrist who classified psychopaths as 'non-sane, non-insane.' That doesn't make sense either -- yet in a way, it does.

One thing is certain — psychopathy is a perplexing disorder.

Here's what one anonymous psychopath has to say about it:

"It's funny because 'inside' is much more chaotic than I show. It is an interesting paradox because inside my head I am positively insane but 'outside' my head I am perfectly normal (when need be)…There are two people in my head and they both think differently. One controls my thoughts and the other, my actions….The one who controls my thoughts tries to sway me one way or the other, but ultimately I decide who's argument has the most merit. In reality, insanity is only characterized by your actions.

Having voices in your head doesn't make you crazy; following their will in a public setting leading to incarceration does."

ABOUT THE AUTHOR

AB Admin is the pen name for the author of the unique and popular website, Psychopaths and Love.

She has written several books:

Psychopaths and Love

Boundaries: Loving Again After a Pathological Relationship

30 Covert Emotional Manipulation Tactics

202 Ways To Spot a Psychopath in Personal Relationships

www.psychopathsandlove.com

23304533R00097

Made in the USA
Middletown, DE
21 August 2015